Being a Teacher

Sharing the stories of educators working in a diverse range of international contexts, *Being a Teacher* uses personal narratives to explore effective teaching and learning in global settings. Demonstrating how personal values influence pedagogical practice, and asking how practice can be improved, authors reflect on their experiences not just as teachers, but also as learners, to offer essential guidance for all prospective educational professionals.

The book focuses on teacher narratives as a vehicle for consideration of teacher professionalism, and as a way of understanding issues which are important to teachers in different contexts. By sharing and analysing these narratives, the book discusses the increasing complexity of teaching as a profession, and considers the commonality within the narratives. Each chapter includes graphic representations of analysis and encourages its reader to reflect critically on central questions, thereby constructing their own narrative.

Being a Teacher provides an in-depth and engaging insight into the education system at a global level, making it an essential read for anyone embarking on a teaching career within the international education market.

Lucy Cooker is Course Leader for the International Postgraduate Certificate in Education at Nottingham University, UK.

Tony Cotton writes widely on education for learners and teachers. He is currently working with educators in Brazil, Jamaica and Macedonia as well as being a tutor on the International Postgraduate Certificate in Education at Nottingham University, UK.

Helen Toft is Lead Tutor on the International Postgraduate Certificate in Education at Nottingham University, UK, and teaches the Bangkok cohort of the programme.

Being a Teacher

Teaching and Learning in
a Global Context

Lucy Cooker, Tony Cotton and
Helen Toft

Routledge
Taylor & Francis Group

LONDON AND NEW YORK

First published 2018
by Routledge
2 Park Square, Milton Park, Abingdon, Oxon OX14 4RN

and by Routledge
711 Third Avenue, New York, NY 10017

Routledge is an imprint of the Taylor & Francis Group, an informa business

British Library Cataloguing-in-Publication Data
A catalogue record for this book is available from the British
Library

Library of Congress Cataloging-in-Publication Data
Names: Cotton, Tony, author. | Cooker, Lucy, 1970- author. |
Toft, Helen, author.
Title: Being a teacher: teaching and learning in a global
context / Tony Cotton, Lucy Cooker and Helen Toft.
Description: Abingdon, Oxon; New York, NY: Routledge,
2018. | Includes bibliographical references.
Identifiers: LCCN 2017047074 | ISBN 9781138207073 (hbk) |
ISBN 9781138207080 (pbk) | ISBN 9781315463179 (ebk)
Subjects: LCSH: Education and globalization. | International
education. | Reflective teaching.
Classification: LCC LC191.C587 2018 | DDC 371.14/4–dc23
LC record available at https://lccn.loc.gov/2017047074

ISBN: 9781138207073 (hbk)
ISBN: 9781138207080 (pbk)
ISBN: 9781315463179 (ebk)

Typeset in Bembo
by Sunrise Setting Ltd, Brixham, UK

MIX
Paper from
responsible sources
FSC
www.fsc.org   FSC™ C013985

Printed in the United Kingdom
by Henry Ling Limited

Contents

Preface

By talking through what it was that made teachers inspiring for us we discovered what it is that can make us inspiring teachers.

Writing the book forced me to question and acknowledge just how much my schooling affected me and made me the teacher I am today.

As our histories unraveled we discovered shared experiences I would never have imagined.

These three quotations come from the cover of a book called *Thinking about Teaching* (Cotton 1998). This book explored the stories of eight educators working in a wide range of settings. Tony who edited the book, and Helen, who was one of the contributors, remember the process of writing as formative in their own thinking about teaching. However, the world of education in 1998 was very different from the world we inhabit today.

The education system is becoming a global system. International comparisons rate country against country and governments send ministers and education advisers on visits around the world to try to capture the holy grail of what makes effective teaching and learning. Similarly, teaching is becoming increasingly globalised. A recent report from the British Council suggested that, 'There is a fast-moving worldwide shift from English being taught as a foreign language (EFL) to English being the medium of instruction (EMI)' (Dearden 2015).

It felt like time to revisit *Thinking about Teaching*, placing the exploration of what it is that makes a 'teacher' in a global context.

This new book shares and analyses narratives from educators working across a diverse range of international contexts. The authors, who have experienced education in many different countries and are now teaching around the world, reflect on their experiences as learners and as teachers. Their personal stories of individual educational journeys share the belief that education is a force for change within individuals and across continents. Our stories offer the view that teaching and learning are ultimately a shared human experience with relationships at the heart of all learning. Through reading and engaging with these stories we hope that you will be supported on your journey to become the best teacher you can be.

We aim to provide an in-depth and engaging insight into the education system at a global level and hope that anyone thinking about beginning a teaching career across the international education system will find it useful. Our aim here is to support you in seeing these insights embodied in your own and others' practice and to offer a critique of an over simplistic 'one-size-fits-all' notion of teacher effectiveness. We also invite you to construct your own personal vision for the future, both in terms of the types of school you would like to teach in and the type of teacher you would wish to become. We do this through encouraging you to reflect on your own thinking and to add your own stories to the book by using it as a personal journal. In this sense, the book will become your own 'commonplace book'. We will discuss the idea of a commonplace book in much more detail in Chapter 1. For now, it is sufficient to quote Virginia Woolf, who describes a commonplace book as

> one of those old notebooks which we have all, at one time or another, had a passion for beginning. Most of the pages are blank, it is true; but at the beginning we shall find a certain number very beautifully covered with a strikingly legible hand-writing. Here we have written down the names of great writers in their order of merit; here we have copied out fine passages from the classics; here are lists of books to be read; and here, most interesting of all, lists of books that have actually been read, as the reader testifies with some youthful vanity by a dash of red ink.
>
> (Woolf 1958: 25)

The three authors who have edited the book met while working on the University of Nottingham's Post Graduate Certificate of Education (International) (PGCEi) course and teaching in Bangkok. This course, which offers an education qualification to teachers working in international schools that teach through the medium of English, has become one of the biggest education courses in the university. The Bangkok cohort is one of 21 from across the globe. There is a small amount of face-to-face teaching followed by a year of online study. The authors' experience of working with these beginning teachers from many different countries convinced them of the need for this book. Many of the participants on the PGCEi course begin the programme with the belief that education can be a force for social change. Similarly, even though they have learned in many different countries and are teaching in vastly different social and political contexts, they share an understanding that personal values and beliefs are at the heart of schooling and education.

So, who are the authors who will share their stories with you? The three authors who have edited the book are Lucy, Tony and Helen. Lucy is the course leader for the PGCEi. This course runs in 15 countries giving Lucy vast experience of the international education context. Lucy started her career teaching English in Japan before completing her PhD which explored issues in language teaching back at Nottingham University. She is currently carrying out research in a range of schools around the world many of which follow the International Baccalaureate (IB) curriculum.

Tony is a writer and educational consultant. Previously he has been Head of the School of Education and Childhood at Leeds Metropolitan University; programme leader for the BA Primary Education at Nottingham Trent University; and course leader for the PGCE Mathematics at Nottingham University. His most recent publications include two books for Routledge: *Understanding and Teaching Primary Mathematics*, 3rd edition (2016); and *Teaching for Mathematical Understanding – Practical ideas for outstanding lessons* (2016). He is the lead author for *Oxford International Primary Mathematics* (Oxford University Press, 2014), a mathematics programme for international schools; and recently edited *Towards an Education for Social Justice: Ethics applied to education* for Peter Lang publishers (2012). He writes regularly in the professional press including the *Times Educational Supplement* and for the journal *Mathematics Teaching*. He has worked with teachers and beginning teachers in 21 countries over the last 18 years.

Helen has taught for many years in English secondary and primary schools, usually through the medium of experiential or process drama. More recently she has taught on education degree courses to young and more mature adults wanting to deepen their understanding of teaching for personal and professional development in England and South East Asia, many from culturally diverse backgrounds and experiences. One course which was most significant in her development was running a bespoke taster course at Leeds Metropolitan University, now Leeds Beckett, for teachers who had escaped conflict in their country and come to the UK as refugees and asylum seekers. Supporting their journey to become fully qualified teachers in and around Leeds became a passion to support multicultural classrooms in and around the city. Currently Helen has been delighted to join the team delivering the PGCEi course in Bangkok for Nottingham University.

The lead author team were joined by six co-authors who worked closely with them in exploring their life histories through often very different experiences of education. These co-authors are

Edward Emmett: Born and educated in London, UK. Currently lives and teaches at a school in Bangkok, Thailand. Has responsibility for early years education within the school.

Lisa Fernandes: Born and educated in Bangalore, India. Has lived and worked in Oman and Canada. Currently teaching in the primary section of an international school in Bangalore.

Cassius Lubisi: Born and educated in South Africa. Completed his PhD in Nottingham, UK. Currently secretary to the President of South Africa.

Haana Sandy: Born and educated in Iran. Currently lives and works as a secondary teacher of mathematics in the UK.

Jarret (known as J) Voytilla: Born and educated in Canada. Has worked in Mexico and currently lives in Thailand. Teaches at 'The Global School', a US institution which moves around the world relocating to a new country every semester.

Han Wei: Born and educated in China. Has worked in Mauritius, China and the UK. Currently studying for a Masters degree in England and teaching Mandarin in the Chinese community in Manchester.

We will finish this brief preface as Tony and Helen finished the preface in *Thinking about Teaching*, with a quote from bell hooks which offers an aim for all our work and an analysis of the writing process.

When we commit ourselves to education as the practice of freedom, we participate in the making of an academic community where we can be and become intellectuals in the fullest and deepest sense of the word. We participate in a way of learning and being that makes the world more rather than less real, one that enables us to live fully and freely. This is the joy in our quest.

(hooks 1999: 72)

Acknowledgements

The process of writing this book, with a global team of co-authors, has been an absolute joy for all of us. The openness and inspiration of each member of the team has led to a book that inspires us even as we read it back. It is genuinely a book written through collaboration, so the first thanks are from each member of the ten-strong writing and graphicing team to each other. We couldn't have done it alone.

We must thank Dr. Paul Thompson, who designed and developed the PGCEi in collaboration with other colleagues at the University of Nottingham, and therefore, gave all of us the opportunity to work on such an interesting programme. We would also like to say thank you to all our colleagues who currently work on the programme and with whom we share ideas about the development of international education. Perhaps most importantly we acknowledge the contribution of all the students on the course, particularly those on the Bangkok cohorts where we teach together, as well as those from all around the world, who make teaching and learning such an enthralling endeavour.

Finally, we would like to pay a huge thank you to our colleague and best of friends, Eddy Walton, who has brought her expansive creativity to our process by visualising how the stories connected at the end of each chapter. She is also responsible for the amazing image on the cover of the book. From the outset Eddy and the writing team recognised something in each other's approach to teaching which illuminated possibilities for all.

Lucy, Tony and Helen

Part 1

Introductions

Chapter 1

Introduction

We described in the preface how this book grew out of our shared experience teaching on the PGCEi, a qualification for teachers in international schools. Many of the participants on this course have come to teaching as a way of funding their travels or, once they have found a place to settle in, or a person to settle with, they have taken to teaching as a way of supporting their new family life. This is not to say that teaching is entirely functional for them, is simply a way of making money; on the contrary many participants have started in language support or teaching English as a second language and realised that teaching is the job for them.

One of the many joys of working with these participants is that there is no common shared experience of education systems or assumed norms of pedagogical approaches. For example, the group of participants Tony is currently working with attended school in seven different countries and are teaching in five different countries. This diversity of experience brings a richness to the discussions that does not often appear in UK-based courses which tend to have a much more homogenous group of participants.

There is one shared understanding among the participants on the PGCEi and this is that a teaching qualification is a licence to travel. For them, teaching has become a truly global profession.

Teaching as a global profession

Teaching now transcends geographical barriers. As you read the book you will explore in detail one fascinating example of this: a school that literally transcends national barriers by relocating to a new country every term. *THINK Global School* combines what is described as a high-quality curriculum with world travel. This year the students will attend a school located in Peru for the first term of the year before relocating to Morocco for the second term and finishing the academic year in Canada. The school website describes life for the students in the following way:

> At THINK Global School, the diversity of your meals is the perfect metaphor for student life. While no two days are quite the same, you can always count on being part of a small, close-knit community devoted to supporting and nurturing each other through the experience of attending high school abroad. Along the way you'll travel the globe, live like locals, and share your experiences with friends old and new. It's a revolutionary system of living and learning where no moment goes un-savored and your education comes alive in the everyday.
>
> (http://thinkglobalschool.org/student-life/)

It takes a particular type of teacher to work in this way. J. will describe his life and work in detail throughout the book but imagine having the flexibility to teach in a new country every term and having to find ways to connect your teaching to the specifics of the new environment you find yourself in; the new set of authors and artists you can connect with and the new scientific and mathematical cultures that you can draw on in your lessons. It is no wonder that the website sees those who are 'lean-forward learners who never stop asking questions' as potential teachers.

While *THINK Global School* is an extreme example of the global nature of teaching and learning many schools in the UK are examples of the shrinking global world in which we live. Data from the Department of Education suggests that over 300 languages are spoken in schools in the UK. The demographic make-up of many schools has changed considerably over the last decade to reflect the increasingly diverse society in which we live.

But although teaching has become a global profession and schools are having to develop to serve a more diverse range of learners learning has not become a global right.

The movement of people around the world is at its greatest reported level. At the time of writing it is estimated that 65 million people have been displaced from their homes. This is just under 1 per cent of the

Table 1.1 Current provision of education globally

	Low-income countries	*Middle-income countries*	*High-income countries*
Will not learn basic primary level skills	69%	21%	8%
Will learn only basic primary level skills	23%	30%	22%
Will learn minimum secondary level skills	8%	49%	70%

Source: Education Commission projections (2016).

world's population. It is also the equivalent of the whole population of the UK being on the move. As many as 21.3 million of these displaced persons are refugees escaping persecution or running for their lives from war that has engulfed them and their families.

A report from the Global Education Commission entitled *The Learning Generation: Investing in Education for a Changing World* offers an analysis in Table 1.1 of the current state of global education.

The report suggests that £23 billion is required to ensure all children have access to primary and secondary education by 2030. Their global education plan has the following set of objectives:

- Quality preschool education is accessible for all children.
- All girls and boys will complete primary school and all ten-year-olds will have functional literacy and numeracy skills.
- The proportion of girls and boys achieving secondary level skills in low-income countries will reach levels current in high-income countries.
- Participation in post-secondary learning in low-income countries will be close to the levels seen today in high-income countries.
- Inequalities in participation and learning between the richest and poorest children within countries will be sharply reduced, coupled with strong progress in reducing other forms of inequality.

This aim for full access to primary and secondary education for all updates and develops the Millennium Goal for education. Target 2A is that the world should aim to achieve universal primary education and that by 2015, children everywhere, boys and girls alike, will be able to complete a full course of primary schooling.

Since this target was set there have been improvements in the educational experience for many children. For example:

- Enrolment in primary education in developing regions reached 91 per cent in 2015, up from 83 per cent in 2000.
- Among youth aged 15 to 24, the literacy rate improved globally from 83 per cent to 91 per cent between 1990 and 2015 and the gap between women and men has narrowed.

However, there is still a considerable distance to travel before these aims can be seen to have been fully met. For example:

- In 2015, 57 million children of primary school age were out of school.
- In the developing regions, children in the poorest households are four times as likely to be out of school as those in the richest households.
- In countries affected by conflict, the proportion of out-of-school children increased from 30 per cent in 1999 to 36 per cent in 2012.
  (Data retrieved from www.un.org/millenniumgoals)

While the focus of this book is the stories of teachers around the world we should not forget that tied up in teachers' stories are learners' stories. One of the aspirations for all those engaged in international teacher education is that a teaching workforce with an understanding of the global impact of education can become change agents to work for a more equitable experience of education around the world. Only global educators can make the Millennium target 2A a reality.

Teaching is a global profession and teachers around the world have stories to tell and connections to make. These connections can serve to make us all more effective teachers and can support us in our quest to develop an education system which all children can access and which is a first step in creating a more equal and just global society.

The development of international schools

A recent report by the International Schools Consultancy (ISC) suggests that the number of international kindergarten-to-Grade-12 schools has increased by over 40 per cent in the last five years. They estimate the current total number of such international schools to be 8,257 attended by over 4.3 million pupils. The largest increase has been in Asia (including Western Asia and the Middle East) with a 55.7 per cent growth in the number of students.

This would suggest that more families are choosing to pay to send their children to international schools to learn through the medium of English as this will allow their children access to globally recognised qualifications whether this be the International Baccalaureate, qualifications gained through the Cambridge International Examinations organisation or the Scholastic Assessment Tests (SATs) and the American College Testing (ACT) from the United States. It also suggests that western pedagogical approaches may be becoming favoured by some groups of parents.

While this growth of international schools continues local national curricula will become influenced by the curriculum adopted by the international schools and by the pedagogical approaches that they espouse. International schools are seen as high-status institutions even though the quality and standards in such schools can vary widely. International schools are no longer the home for children of ex-pats, diplomats and government officials exclusively but attract an increasing number of 'host country nationals' (students who are from the country in which the school is located).

This growth of international schools has been followed by an expansion of university-based teacher education provision internationally. The course based at the University of Nottingham out of which this book grew now runs in 15 locations around the world. It has nearly 1,000 students currently on the programme, which makes it the biggest teacher education course in the university.

Over the last 20 years, teacher education has become increasingly professionalised and now regards itself as a rigorous academic discipline with a long history of research and development. This has led to an increased global understanding of the issues and problems within education and teacher education and a shared commitment to engaging with the difficult questions that are thrown up by learning and teaching across the world. The American Educational Research Association (AERA) annual conference in 2016 was attended by nearly 16,000 delegates and the AERA President, Joyce E. King, discussed the universal human right to education and the moral obligation of educators and educational researchers to work for the benefit of oppressed groups around the world.

This increasing globalisation of teacher education means that aims and beliefs of the curricula emanating from the UK, the United States and Australia are becoming increasingly close.

Aims and beliefs of international curricula

A programme which is followed in over 4,500 international schools is the International Baccalaureate (IB). The IB was founded in 1968 although the current programme was developed from a framework laid down by Marie-Therese Maurette who worked in the international school in Geneva. She published her framework in a 1948 UNESCO booklet *Educational Techniques for Peace. Do They Exist?* In terms of a shared purpose for global education this seems like an appropriate starting point. The current IB mission states that their aim is to 'create a better world through education'. One of the ways that the curriculum on offer in IB schools works towards this aim is to ask all teachers in all lessons to develop a set of skills and attributes in their learners. These skills and attributes are listed as a set of learner profiles. This learner profile states that all students in IB schools should become:

- Inquirers through developing their natural curiosity.
- Knowledgeable through exploring concepts that have local and global significance.
- Thinkers exercising initiative in thinking critically and creatively.
- Communicators who understand and express ideas and information confidently.
- Principled – acting with integrity and honesty.
- Open-minded – understanding their own cultures and personal histories.
- Caring – showing empathy, compassion and respect to the needs and feelings of others.
- Risk-takers approaching unfamiliar situations and uncertainties with courage and forethought.
- Balanced – understanding the importance of intellectual, physical and emotional balance.
- Reflective – giving thoughtful consideration to their own learning and experience.

To conclude the book we will develop a set of teacher competencies which we argue will support the development of a global education system acting for social justice. Before that point, it may be worth pausing for a moment and reflecting for yourself.

In contrast to the far-reaching and international aim of the IB programme the UK National Curriculum introduced in 2014 has the stated aim that the national curriculum should provide pupils with 'an introduction to the essential knowledge that they need to be educated citizens'. This rather modest aim, that the curriculum is only an introduction, continues to state that the curriculum 'introduces pupils to the best that has been thought and said; and helps engender an appreciation of human creativity and achievement'.

This statement of aims raises several questions. What knowledge is 'essential', indeed how might we define an 'educated citizen'? Or are the two ideas directly linked? An educated citizen is one who has all the essential knowledge necessary and vice-versa. For a global educator the statement is disappointing as it perhaps suggests education is seen purely in terms of knowledge and of passing on knowledge in the hope that it may help pupils come to an appreciation of creativity. This aim stands in stark contrast to the aims of the IB curriculum discussed earlier and suggests that the UK curriculum may not be as influential on the international stage as it once was.

An interim report for *The Primary Review* undertaken for Cambridge University by Maha Shuayb and Sharon O'Donnell, *Aims and Values in Primary Education: England and Other Countries*, describes the ways in which the curricula in six countries have developed over the last 40 years. They notice a tension between two ideas, child-centred education, and social and economic progress within the country. We would argue that this latter point has become emphasised in recent years through the growth of international comparative testing. The conclusions in the report suggest that child-centred philosophies were particularly clear in the 1960s and 1970s in England, Scotland and New Zealand but that optimism that education might bring about social change in terms of greater equality was overtaken by the argument that education should be seen as a tool for economic development. The authors argue that the influence of child-centred pedagogical approaches maintained an influence throughout the 1980s and 1990s in Germany and the Netherlands.

We wonder if this tension is visible in developing countries as they augment their education system alongside emerging democratic institutions. Initially there is a sense that education can be emancipatory and can equip learners to become active citizens. However, as economic development takes hold the call for education to drive the economy and take on more functional forms becomes more dominant. This tension takes us into the final section of this chapter.

What is education for?

In a sense this is the question that underpins the book. Through exploring our stories we come to an answer about what we, as individuals, think education is for. By analysing these stories we can offer a global vision of what education is for, which in turn allows us to ask: what kinds of teachers are needed in such a system? We can then turn this question back on ourselves and ask: what do I need to change to become the best teacher I can be within this system?

We want to finish this chapter with the opening activity on the Nottingham University PGCEi course. Participants are asked to watch a video of Pete Seeger performing 'What Did You Learn in School Today?' (1964);[1] available to watch on YouTube.

Note

1   Available on YouTube at www.youtube.com/watch?v=VucczIg98Gw.

Commonplace book: Entry 1

Which of these attributes do you think you develop most effectively in your learners?

Which of these attributes are sidelined in your classroom because of other curriculum pressures or the beliefs inherent in the system in which you work?

What could you do differently to develop these attributes in your students?

Commonplace book: Entry 2

Think back to when you were at school. Try to think about the curriculum both in terms of what you studied and the way in which the curriculum was taught and assessed.

What do you think the aims of the curriculum were?

Do you think it achieved its aims?

What do you think are the aims of the curriculum you currently teach?

How would you describe your own aims for a school curriculum?

Chapter 2

How we wrote this book

How do I know what I think until I see what I say?

(Forster 2005 [1927]: 71)

Tony shared this quote from E. M. Forster with the rest of the author team as we began to think through how we might write this book. It is a quote that he shares with all learners he works with when they begin the process of keeping a journal. And wherever he works with whoever he is working with, whether they are PhD students or four-year-olds, he insists that they keep a journal.

This is because something happens when we write down our thoughts. They cease to be thoughts and become more tangible. We wonder whether we have captured what we 'really' mean, and in that wondering we create new meaning. There may also be an audience, if only an imaginary one, and that audience can ask us about our thinking. In replying to their questions we imbue our writing with new meaning. These ideas informed our process as we put this book together.

The author team and the process

You will meet all the authors in more detail in the next chapter. For now, it is sufficient to know that the three core authors are Helen, Lucy and Tony. You may have noticed that the names appear in alphabetical order. This is deliberate as we want to be clear that there was no hierarchy in the writing. This core team came up with the structure of the book and the plan for creating the finished book. As a group we thought about the many fascinating and inspiring teachers we had worked with over the years and winnowed this group down to a group of six colleagues who could bring their experiences together representing each continent, as many disciplines as possible and as many phases of education as possible. We began by sharing our autobiographies; initially Helen, Lucy and Tony wrote and then shared their writing. We were all tentative, feeling inadequate. Each of us said our story wasn't as interesting as that of our co-authors. Each of us thought the others could turn a better phrase, but through reading aloud we realised that we had something to say.

We then worked with our co-authors to create their autobiographies, some through Skype interviews, some through email, drafting and redrafting until we were both happy that we were telling our stories as we wanted. The process of 'seeing what we were saying' allowed us to unpick what we were thinking.

This process was repeated for each chapter in the book. First the core team would write and share their stories and then the process would be repeated with the teams of co-authors. We found that reading aloud became an important part of the process. Once we had gathered all the stories for each chapter we would take it in turns to read them aloud. We did not read our own stories out loud or those of our own set of co-authors. Hearing the words that we had written or co-written read by someone else allowed us to hear these stories as a reader might read them. This in turn helped us to ask questions of each other's writing to redraft them and pick out the details seen (or heard) as important by fresh ears.

Once a chapter had been put together another important person came into the mix: Eddie, who has produced the graphics at the end of each chapter. We would take it in turns to read sections of the chapter and Eddie would graphic the key points that were emerging from the stories. She is skilled at noticing the commonalities and the key themes that emerge from stories. These graphics form an important record of our thinking and we hope that this form of analysis allows you to notice critical moments in the stories too.

Autobiographical writing

To support us in our writing we started with a series of questions. For example, the questions that we used to structure our autobiographies in the next chapter were:

- Who are you?
- What has influenced your direction in life?

- What were the most meaningful parts of your education?
- How did education fit in with the values held at home?
- What are the international dimensions of your life?
- What are your hopes for those that you work with?

We asked each other the first questions repeatedly until we ran out of answers to 'Who are you?' This allowed us to start from a view of ourselves as having multiple identities. We then spent time on our own written responses to the other questions before coming back together and reading our early drafts aloud. At this point we would ask each other to develop certain ideas, to tell the stories in more depth. When we are writen for ourselves we tend to skip over important detail, as suggested above; when we read aloud our audience can ask for the detail to be clarified. We would repeat this process until we were all satisfied that there was a depth to our writing which would allow us to get inside and underneath the stories. This is where the analysis starts.

We repeated this process for each chapter; honing and refining the vignettes until they really revealed what it was we wanted to say.

Learning from experience

A colleague of mine used to say, 'The one thing that we don't seem to learn from experience is how to learn from experience'. As you will have realised we set great store in learning from experience. This is often described as becoming a 'reflective practitioner'. It is common to find an aim of a teacher education course as developing 'reflective' teachers. This idea underpins the book as it consists of the author team's reflections on their educational journey of reflections on what these experiences have taught us.

Reflection can be seen as turning something over in your mind. Not just letting thoughts pass through our minds but almost literally turning them over to see what they reveal; selecting a particular moment and exploring it in depth to analyse what it reveals. This helps us reformulate our ideas and gives us new ways of looking at things. We can then compare our reflections with those of our colleagues. This reformulation helps us connect different events in our lives and different ideas we have so that we can see connecting structures within our thoughts and actions. Most importantly, perhaps, reflecting helps us learn how to best use our personal experience to develop in the future. This allows us to become more in control of the way we think and act. We begin to act in particular ways because we have made a conscious decision to do so, we feel more comfortable about the way we operate and so feel more in control of our lives. We hope that this process of thinking carefully about the issues raised in the book will make you better equipped to learn from your own experience in the future.

Reflecting on experience

Reflecting on critical moments in our educational life can help in other ways. It can help us explore the reasons why learners may behave in particular ways in particular situations. It can help us explore how the way that we work as teachers produces a particular response from our learners. It may also help us figure out how to work most effectively with colleagues and how to avoid conflict. The 'vignettes' or 'little stories' that you will read may challenge something that you have previously thought to be true, may challenge your current common-sense view of the world and in this way may begin to rewrite your world. One of the advantages of drawing on a range of authors from diverse backgrounds and working in a wide range of contexts is that it becomes clear that there are several sides to every story. Truth becomes multifaceted.

We hope that the vignettes we share with you present teaching and learning as a human activity. We hope they prioritise emotions, that they foreground our humanity and allow us to see both teachers and learners as human beings. Finally, we hope that the vignettes help you in your own hypothesising. They invite you to wonder, 'what would I have done in that situation?'; 'How might I have acted differently?' Perhaps most importantly we hope that you are challenged to ask, 'Would I have acted like that, in that situation?'

What is in the book?

The book is in four parts. In Part I we set the context for your reading and introduce you to the author team. We hope that this allows you to develop an understanding of who we are and what we believe. We would expect different readers to follow different authors whose stories resonate with you. We also invite you to begin your own educational autobiography in this section.

Part 2 of the book focuses on the authors' experiences as learners in the range of contexts in which they were educated. Chapter 4 explores a typical day in the educational life of each author. These vignettes illustrate the huge differences in the contexts in which we work while drawing together the similarities in terms of the aims and beliefs of education. We then explore our 'best' teachers. We hope that these vignettes illustrate the many different contexts within which the authors were educated themselves. The analysis of the narratives begins to explore what it is that makes an effective teacher.

We then move on to explore the lessons we have learned through narratives which focus on the negative experiences that all the authors have had at some stage in their learning. Through analysing these experiences we show that we can learn educational lessons from even the most painful experiences. Finally, we explore our motivations to succeed. Here the author team reflect on the role models or other individuals that kept them going in moments of crisis or loss of confidence. All educators learn to become resilient; this chapter explores how we learn to do this.

Part 3 moves on to explore and analyse our experiences as teachers – initially, by describing the 'best' teachers we have worked with. Through analysing the detailed and rich descriptions of these teachers in action we aim to get underneath what makes a great teacher. This is developed to show how we have learned the lessons from our own best teachers to allow us to teach excellent lessons ourselves. Our interpretation of what makes an excellent lesson also reveals much about our fundamental aims and beliefs for our subject and for education.

The final part, Part 4, describes our shared vision for education by drawing together the analysis from each chapter to offer a shared vision of a global educational system and a global teacher. The closing chapter, Chapter 11, asks, 'What makes a global educator?' In this chapter, we share the results of a virtual workshop which allowed all the authors to develop a set of competencies which the team think define a global educator.

How to use the book

As we suggested above we expect that different readers will read the book differently. You may select a particular author to follow or you may find different parts of the book more engaging or more relevant to your current interests or questions. We would suggest that you engage with the ideas in the book by writing yourself. This is why we have included boxes in which you are invited to respond to your reading. This is a book in which you are expected to write.

We would also invite you to make the reading of the book collaborative to reflect the way we have written the book. Read sections aloud to a colleague. Share your writing. Explore the graphics at the end of each chapter with a group of friends or colleagues to come to a shared view as to the key issues in each chapter. Most importantly we would encourage you to keep a commonplace book as you read. Buy yourself a new book, a new pen or pencil, and whenever you are reading have them to hand.

Keeping a commonplace book

In many ways this book can be seen as extracts from our commonplace books over a shared 300 years in education. We understand that the idea of keeping a commonplace book as you read may seem like hard work, may seem to add to the burden of a busy life as a teacher; but as the book is all about thinking over what it is that has made us educators we invite you to join us in thinking about what kind of educator you may become in the future. We suggest that this will pay off for several reasons.

As we said in the opening of the chapter writing helps us learn because when we commit something to the page we think about it in a different way. In some sense you have to believe in what you write and give your thoughts more attention than if you leave them unwritten. Writing also allows you to revisit your thoughts at a later date and re-examine them to see if you still think in the same way. This may sometimes be embarrassing, but it is always useful to look back on the ways we used to think and compare these ideas to how we think now.

More pragmatically, for those readers embarking on teacher education courses, it is likely that you will be asked to keep a record of your experiences as a teacher. You may be asked by your tutors to 'reflect' on your experiences as a newly beginning teacher, to analyse your actions and to offer alternative interpretations to the observations you make during your course. This is a skill to be learned and developed as you move through the course and your career. We hope that by using this book as you begin your career we will support you in developing these skills. Through writing responses to the questions we pose you may find it easier to uncover what you actually think about teaching and learning. Your own values and beliefs will become clearer.

In addition to being a place to write down your reflections your commonplace book should be a repository for anything which you read or see that impacts on your reflections. Were any of the author team to sit opposite you on a train and see a copy of this book filled with your jottings; with articles from newspapers stuck between the pages; with pages added which contain your sketches or images that you have found on the web and with additional quotations from other reading you have been doing we would consider the book a huge success.

Now it is time to meet the authors.

Chapter 3

Who are we?

Whenever starting work with a new group of learners it is important to establish a feeling of trust. Your group needs to know where you, the teacher, are coming from, what your beliefs and values are. And they need to know this from the very beginning of the relationship so that they get a feeling for what to expect as they work with you. In a similar way, at the beginning of the process of writing the book we needed to get a feel for each other. We needed to discover what values we shared and what made us different. What follows is the result of this process. We hope that these autobiographies allow you to connect with us. As you read this section you may want to underline or highlight things that strike you as particularly relevant to you or things that you find surprising.

Lucy Cooker

I'm Lucy Cooker (as in 'oven'). I am 46 and a partner, daughter, sister, auntie and dog owner. And I am an educator. I would rather not call myself a teacher because I have never taught in a school and for most of my career I have not stood in front of a class of students in a typical teacher role.

An important part of my identity is my partner, Claire, and the fact I'm in a same sex relationship. I identify less easily with the term 'lesbian'. I fell in love with someone who happened to be a woman. I have spent many years of my professional life feeling wary of being open about Claire. For example, I have resisted having photos of her on my office noticeboard. However, the processes of self-editing which many gay people engage in, for example, remembering to use gender neutral pronouns and to avoid talking about what one is doing at the weekend, are tiring ones. It is an important and enjoyable part of teaching to be able to share who you are, to tell anecdotes about your life and to feel authentic in your voice. Therefore, recently, I have made the decision to be explicit about this important aspect of my life. I hope that by doing so I can be a role-model for other teachers whose lives do not follow a conventional pattern.

The other important part of my identity is that of traveller. From my first solo trip overseas at age 12, to the extensive and varied travelling that is part of my professional and personal life today I have enjoyed engaging with different people and different cultures.

I am typical of many teaching families in that both my parents were teachers. My mum had been an early years teacher but, like many women of her generation, had given up teaching when I was born. My dad was a head teacher at primary level. For many years, I resisted identifying with this teaching background and believed I would never become a teacher. Thus, I did not enter education as a profession through a teacher education route. Instead, I ended up as an educator through following a Teaching English as a Foreign Language (TEFL) qualification. The dreams and potential of travel were the drivers for that route. I shared a dream of travelling and living overseas with my boyfriend at the time. We completed the Cambridge Certificate in Teaching English to Speakers of Other Languages (CELTA) course together. The relationship didn't last, but the course set me on a trajectory of teaching and travelling which has remained fundamental to my life ever since. International travel is also a part of my family history. My mum had lived in Paris and worked as a nanny. Then she went on exchange as a teacher to New Zealand for a year in the 1960s when this required a six-week journey by boat. Previously, my mum's brother had emigrated to New Zealand and my dad's brother to the United States, so I had an international world of cousins.

I was always a good girl at school. I did my homework and I behaved in class. Education was important, especially school-based education. To be a 'good person' was important with a strong moral (but non-religious) underpinning. In addition to school, my sister and I had rich learning lives and were encouraged in extra-curricular activities such as music lessons, chess, swimming, gymnastics and ballet. Dad came from a working-class background. He was the youngest of four children and was the first in his family to attend a grammar school. Eventually he became a teacher through attending Goldsmiths' Teacher Training

College. He's always had a passion for state education. My mum failed the entrance examination for grammar school so her parents paid for her to attend a convent school, which she hated. However, this was very powerful in terms of her belief in non-selective education, so when I was aged 9 we moved from Kent to Norfolk so my sister and I could avoid having to take the entrance examination.

My memories of my own school life are mixed. At primary school, I remember being forced to stand up and then sit down when mental arithmetic problems were answered correctly. I was always the last one standing. This has had a lasting influence, and still to this day, I don't know my multiplication tables. At secondary school I did well. I was head girl and I loved French and history. French felt exotic and an escape from the real world. History politicised me, and I became a feminist through learning about the suffragettes and a democrat through learning about the Chartists. I did very badly in my examinations in my final year at school as I enjoyed socialising and rebelled against my parents' control over my life. I refused to retake these examinations and I was offered and accepted a place at Newcastle upon Tyne Polytechnic to read psychology. Newcastle upon Tyne was not a top university (in fact it wasn't even a university) and consequently I still have feelings of a lack of self-worth connected to those times.

After graduating and working for a few years, I went to live in Japan. I felt at home, perhaps because both the UK and Japan are island countries and so there are similar levels of reserve and politeness between the two, although in many other respects Japan and the UK are very different and this was appealing to me too. There was a feeling of liberation living somewhere so different and I felt that I was finally escaping a restriction on my life that I had always felt; from school, from teachers and from my parents.

In this sense, Japan opened my eyes to a world of travel and an accompanying sense of freedom. Now my work takes me travelling for teaching and research and is a fundamental part of who I am and how I see myself. For example, recently I've visited China, Malaysia, Thailand, Peru, US, Laos, Kenya, Portugal, France, Ghana and India for pleasure, teaching and research. I am writing this in April before the UK votes in the EU referendum in June, and this is hugely significant for me. If we leave and become an isolationist nation I know I will feel bereft. I want to be part of a bigger world. In general terms, I feel trapped and have itchy feet if I have no travel planned.

Feeling excited by travel and learning to understand and exist in different cultures allows me to identify with many of the international teachers with whom I work. I hope through my role as an educator they can feel the confidence and professionalism that was not available to me. I also feel excited about sharing the world of international education with colleagues and helping them to experience what learning and teaching means in different cultures. With my 'research hat' on, I hope the participants in the research projects I'm involved with understand that what they do is valued through the research process. I hope that they gain a sense of value from their own understanding.

Tony Cotton

These days I call myself a writer. I spend most of my working days in my shed at the bottom of the garden. I write books for teachers and books for students, sometimes about mathematics and sometimes about education in general. When I'm writing these books I'm Tony Cotton. Sometimes I write short stories or review gigs. When I do this I'm Ant Cotton. I've used two names ever since I started teaching 45 years ago. I quite like separating the two parts of my life in this way.

I have always written. As a young boy, I used to carefully make my own books, stapling the blank pages together before I began my latest story. Part of me enjoys the anticipation after a piece of my writing goes out into the world. I like the sense that once something is published I have no control over what might happen to it. My favourite response to a piece of my writing was from a good friend, Pete. He messaged me to say that he had been at his local barber's reading a magazine. In the magazine was a review of a band called The Fall at a local venue. As he was reading it he said that he thought 'This review is interesting' and that he looked down to see who had written it, smiling when he realised it was me.

I fell into teaching really. At secondary school my favourite subjects were history and English literature. The subject that I was most successful in was mathematics. When I had to choose my subjects to study for my final two years in school I selected these three subjects only to be told by the head teacher that I had to follow either an arts route or a sciences route. As I was a boy, he suggested that it would be most appropriate for me to do sciences so three years later I found myself on a mathematics degree. I wasn't committed to mathematics at the time and hardly went to lectures. The music scene in Sheffield was very exciting so I immersed myself in that instead. I would spend my days sitting in the university café and keeping up with the lectures by reading the set books and keeping up with the music scene by poring over the music press. I was a solitary student and looking back I think that I have always enjoyed solitude. In primary school I would sit away from the teacher's desk and read my own books carefully disguised in the exercise book we were supposed to be using. My teenage years were spent in my bedroom, reading precociously but with a passion and listening to all the music I could lay my hands on.

I am fortunate that I get to travel through my work. This was another thing that fell into my lap really. I was working at Nottingham University and one of my rules was that I always had my door wedged open unless I was having a private conversation. I noticed someone knocking on the door opposite. I asked if I could I help. The person said that they were looking for 'Mick' who I knew was out that afternoon. I asked them why they were looking for him. They told me that they were from the Czech Republic and had been told that he might be able to help them with a project on assessment and mathematics. I shared my background in mathematics education with the visitor and after two cups of coffee and a closed-door conversation I ended up visiting and working in the Czech Republic for several years. Once I had broken out of the country I realised that this was a fantastic way of learning about myself and about the world. The world suddenly became a much smaller place. Well, smaller for me. I was recently returning home from Macedonia and became aware of how my accident of birth allows me to wave my passport and get on a plane, in contrast to my fellow human beings escaping war who can't move freely to reach a place of safety.

More recently I have become a grandad which is incredibly important to me. Felix is teaching me about how people learn, and making me think about schooling through new eyes. He's teaching me to see the world through the eyes of a three-year-old which is incredibly liberating. I think I feel as though I have time and space to reflect on his learning in a way that I couldn't when my own children were growing up.

Edward Emmett

My name is Edward and I was born in London. I grew up on a 'rough' council estate in South London. I did not enjoy going to school. I got into a lot of fights, and attended one of the most violent and problematic schools in South London.

When I left this school, I was able to choose what I studied at college and really valued this freedom. I studied a Sports Science BTEC (Business and Technology Council) rather than A levels and got a distinction in the bio-mechanics module. I would have liked to study bio-mechanics at degree level but as I did not have a high enough grade in my post-16 English examination I had to opt for an adventure tourism course instead. As this was not what I wanted I managed to change my course once I had started university to leisure management. I thought this would offer more opportunities for a future career. This is going to sound strange for a teacher, but even at university I was a bad student. I never went to lectures. I enjoyed the social life. I had money for the first time in my life from bursaries and from grants to support me as a learner with dyslexia. I also had access to loans and all this helped me to party.

I didn't find out I was dyslexic until I was 19 when my step-mum suggested I got tested for Attention Deficit and Hyperactivity Disorder (ADHD). They found I hadn't got ADHD but that I was dyslexic. I had always struggled with the academic side but going to a school with many students with different issues that hindered learning it was never noticed.

Sport was my saving grace throughout my education. At secondary school lots of my peers were into drug dealing, burglary and street violence but my mates and I just went to school and played football till nine or ten-o'clock at night. Growing up I had problems at home. My mum was a heroin addict. My dad was a musician. When I was ten my mum passed away so I started to live with my dad and my final year in primary school was really good.

I lived with my dad and stepfamily and used to fight constantly with my stepmum. I had this feeling all through secondary school that I was left out. Looking back, I think I was terrible to my stepmum as there was always a place for me in the family. I think I was struggling to find my identity. I grabbed at the chance to get out into the world and go to university. When I finished my degree, I came back home. My stepbrother and stepsisters had always lived at home, but when I returned I felt like there wasn't a place for me there. It felt like a step back.

At that point, I didn't have a job. I would have loved to get one and live near my family because I really love them, but I couldn't see this as an option. During my last year of university I became a leisure organiser for 17-year-olds from around the world who came to London to learn

English. All the teachers on this course lived in Thailand and told me a lot about what it was like and that I should try it. I couldn't see myself being a teacher as I had had bad experiences with most of my teachers during school. However, I realised that I'd never have the money to go abroad so I thought I should just give Thailand a two-month trial. I really enjoyed my first job there and stayed longer than I expected but eventually I thought it was time to try for a job in England. I returned home but couldn't get a fulfilling job. One day, standing holding an advertising board from six-o'clock in the morning for a job, I realised that a month ago I had had a well-paid job in Thailand with my own place to live. So, I applied for a job in a school back in Thailand. I am still at that school six years later.

My best experience of learning was the PGCEi course in Bangkok. It was the first time I had worked hard and done well and I'd paid for it from my own bank account. My tutors cared about me. I'd never had conversations or real feedback on my work ever before. The PGCEi was when I realised I could be a teacher for the rest of my life. At the start of the course I expected to fail, but recently I was offered the early years' coordinator's post because of my success on the course. Currently I can't see myself doing any other job.

I'm close to my dad, really close. He played games with me and taught me things I can still remember, the flags of all the countries and multiplication tables as we walked to school. At secondary school my dad cared about me, not about how well I did at school. At school my best friends were from Italy and another friend about the same age as me was an immigrant from Iran whose mum had died and we became very close. I saw him recently and he is in the police force. We laughed when we realised we both had responsible jobs now while when at school we were in trouble all the time.

One of the great values my family gave me was being accepting to people from all different backgrounds. The household where I was growing up was multicultural; many of my family members speak languages other than English. When I spent some time at agricultural college I found myself in a white community that was really racist. I hated it. I couldn't understand their views, couldn't relate to them. I've seen racism in Thailand too, and some elements here upset me but don't affect me too much.

The main thing I would like my students to be is happy. In the future I hope that they will be able to integrate into a multicultural society and be able to have a positive impact on the world. I have similar values to my parents and really think creativity is important. I hope that my students will all be able to think and express themselves in different ways.

Lisa Fernandes

As a teacher who grew up in the 1970s and went to school in Bangalore I am pleased and excited by the schooling options my children have access to today. The youngest of a large South Indian, Roman Catholic family I went to a private convent school run by American Notre Dame nuns. The university where I studied for my Bachelor of Science degree was a Jesuit-run institution in the heart of the city. Being educated in clergy-run institutions fitted into the values that were held at home. The emphasis there was on discipline and traditional methods of teaching and learning where the teacher was the giver of knowledge and the student the receiver were accepted. When I think back I realise that in university I spent more time out of class than studying, finding the whole process of getting a degree tedious with no connection to my life and a waste of my precious time. I spent some time after university rudderless, dabbling with copywriting and client servicing. I ended up getting a job as a merchandiser in a garment export company, which saw me through the next eight years.

Then, newly married, my husband and I moved to Oman for his job, and I got my first glimpse of the IB programme through a voluntary position at the American British Academy in Muscat. The IB philosophy with its emphasis on an inquiry approach with the aim of creating global citizens influenced my direction. I wanted to be a part of this environment that nurtured and encouraged children to be naturally curious and lead balanced lives. The posting in Oman turned out to be short-lived and we left for Toronto where my first child was born. As recent immigrants, we found it hard to make ends meet and the option of requalifying with the Ontario Board Teaching Certification to become a teacher still seemed a distant ambition. I joined the accounts department of a chemical distributor but still dreamt of becoming a teacher. Impressed by the happy, safe environment in which my daughter learned and her practical application of her knowledge, I made the conscious decision to requalify when I could and change careers.

The chance to do my PGCEi was born out of tragic circumstances when I lost my husband and had to relocate and requalify. It was the most meaningful part of my education, as for the first time in all my years of education, I was interested in what I was learning and practising. The importance of theoretical knowledge, classroom observations, and practising teaching and learning strategies opened up my mind. I found the postgraduate level of academic reading and writing demanding after such a large gap in my studies but it served to fill the huge void that was my loss and helped me to move onwards, into a new exciting space.

With an eye on gaining a teaching position in an international school in Bangalore I decided to then complete the Cambridge Certificate in Teaching English to Speakers of Other Languages (CELTA). I left my children with my sister for a month and went to the British Council in Mumbai where the course was being offered. Again, the CELTA was a rigorous course of study and I came back determined to get a job in an international environment. To my surprise, given the fact that I lacked teaching experience, I got a teaching assistant position at Stonehill International School in Bangalore. I enjoy teaching in what I would call a truly international school with teachers from 15 countries and students from over 30 countries. At one of the only schools in our city to run all three IB programmes, I enjoy putting my learning into meaningful practice.

Next year I will move into the learning support department. Stonehill International School will give me the benefit of free tuition for one of my daughters and I am excited that my six-year-old will have the opportunity to inquire and learn in a stimulating, multicultural, happy and safe environment. I have finally found what I enjoy doing and it is my hope that other institutions support their teachers through this journey of lifelong learning from the theoretical and practical experience of others.

Han Wei

I was born in China and lived there for 21 years. I was an only child and had a very nice childhood in a small town in the province of Chongqing, near the Yangtze River. My mother worked as a secretary for a construction company. My father is an accountant. I went to a state primary school and the education was very focused on tests and exams. It was a very didactic approach to education. We just learned to follow instructions and how to get a good score on the final exam. Unlike many Chinese students today, I didn't have any private tuition because it wasn't popular at that time except for posh families in my home town.

My secondary schooling was also in a state school, one of the best in my home town. I studied nine subjects at Junior High School (JHS): Chinese, mathematics, English, history, geography, physics, chemistry, biology and politics. My senior high school was more enjoyable as my parents decided to send me to the second biggest city in the province and it was a large selective boarding school. There were better facilities in this school and the teachers had strong personalities and were prepared to share their experiences with us. They talked about the importance of education and the need to study hard to get into a good university. Everyone was very motivated and tried to study hard. It was interesting but competitive.

After high school, I attended Sichuan International Studies University and studied teaching Chinese as a second language, encouraged by the popularity of the Confucius Institute which was always being featured in the media. My parents didn't make a choice for me. It's common in China for parents to decide on their children's major but I made my own decision and my parents didn't try to influence me. I thought it would be interesting to share the Chinese culture and language and I wanted to interact with foreigners more. As the university was a language university, it was international and my classmates were very open-minded. Our classes were small and we had many interesting discussions, talking about global issues and exchanging views with students from other countries. This period was a very formative time in my life. The emphasis on language gave me an international focus and enabled me to see the importance of being open-minded. The most meaningful part of my education was when I went to Nottingham to study for my Masters. It was most meaningful because it opened my mind about international life. I started to think about and compare China and the West. For example, the rate of development in China has been fast and people who live in cities have a good standard of life. When I visited villages in the UK I couldn't see obvious differences between the countryside and the cities. Here people have enough resources, and their quality of life is good regardless of where they live. But in China the people who live outside of the city are very poor. In some of the remote countryside, people don't even have internet or fresh running water, and have to commute up to two hours to go to school. One day my classmate asked about the differences between China and the UK. There were so many questions that I hadn't thought about. In discussions with my classmates I developed my critical thinking. This was the most meaningful part because it changed me into another person – I'm different now.

While I was in my fourth year at university I found out about a volunteer programme to send teachers to Mauritius. This was a Chinese government programme organised by Gongqingtuanzhongyang (Institution for Organising Young People), a junior element of the Communist Party. My province, Chongqing, was set up to connect with Mauritius. It was the first time I'd heard about Mauritius and I didn't know anything about the country – only that it was a small island next to Madagascar. I could find very little information. It was only the second year this programme had been running. I couldn't even find very much by searching Baidu as internet searches in China are very restricted. Nevertheless, I decided to apply for the programme. It was quite competitive. I had to take a written exam and have an interview to test my English and Putonghua ability but I was accepted and it was very exciting.

I stayed in Mauritius for one year and spent time in three schools teaching Mandarin. In Mauritius, the spoken language is Mauritian Creole, a French-based language with a combination of English, many African and South Asian languages; the official languages are English and French. The interesting thing is in Mauritius all the text books are written in English but the language of television, supermarkets, newspapers and so on is French. English is used as the medium of instruction in schools, and in primary school each student must choose one oriental language – usually Mandarin Chinese, Tamil, Indian or Urdu. Increasingly, Mandarin is becoming popular as more business is done with China.

My experiences at university motivated me to go to Mauritius. I really enjoyed the teaching and I felt it was fruitful. I was happy to see my students' progress every day: learning new words or singing a song in Mandarin. Every Sunday I worked as a teacher of adult students, aged between 50 and 70. Among the adult students was a couple who were very nice. I was 21 and they looked after me. Every Sunday they picked me up and took me to 'school' and dropped me off. They liked my class because in Mauritius Mandarin teachers rarely have professional knowledge or teaching methods. The way of teaching was also very traditional – just instructions, exercises and rarely any activities. So the lessons they received before were probably quite conventional so it's hard to keep them motivated. As I was passionate about teaching and excited about trying my own ideas on teaching, my lessons have quite a lot of activities. As a result, my lessons were popular. This couple enjoyed my teaching and learning with me and we made more connections. After class, they talked to me and from time to time they invited the whole team to their house. They invited me and my colleagues to a New Year party and we met their son who was working in the UK and was home for Christmas, who is now my husband.

Our contract was only for one year so I went back to China. I tried to apply for teaching jobs in other countries but because I was an only child my parents wanted me to stay in Chongqing. In China, we have very strong ties with our parents. The relationships between parents and children are very different from those in the UK. When we are young, generally we have to listen to our parents and have to obey them in terms of choosing a lifetime job. My parents were strongly of the view that I should apply for a job as a civil servant as it is stable enough and not difficult. They didn't want me to teach Mandarin anymore because most opportunities were overseas and they wanted me to stay close to them. Although they did not really force me to work as a civil servant, I still applied for it because I was not sure what to do and my parents only thought of what was best for me. I found work in the courts and was there for three years. From the first day I started to complain to my parents as I didn't feel that I belonged there. The atmosphere was very different from my previous work environment; everyone was talking politics. I like teaching and I prefer culture to politics. Moreover, it is not an easy job for young people; I regularly had to stay late until midnight, or get up at 5am. I tried my best to work there and I learned a lot. I was asked to take a law exam so I could have more choice and become an assistant judge. I tried to study law, but without interest to motivate me and because I hadn't previously studied law at all, I didn't pass.

The couple who I made friends with in Mauritius visited me every year after I went back to China. They had visited China often, as they owned a shop and they bought things to sell, but it was the first time they visited Chongqing. In the first year they came alone; then the second year they brought their son, Eric. He and I started to keep in touch with each other and slowly became friends, even though he was living in the UK. That was in 2012. It was difficult for us because it was long distance, so we had holidays in countries between China and the UK. Sometimes I went to the UK and sometimes he came to China, but we also visited the Netherlands, Finland and Thailand. That's how we started the relationship and how we kept it going. When we had been together about two years we decided we wanted to move to the next step of the relationship. I was also thinking that I wanted to change my career. I still liked teaching so I decided to quit my job and to study a Masters, this time in the UK, so we could have more time together and get to know each other more. That's how I made the decision to study in the UK. Eric was in Manchester but he visited me in Nottingham at least once a week. We had a great time in both cities. Then after one year we were ready for the next step and during a trip to Edinburgh he proposed to me.

It was very difficult for my parents as I am an only child. They struggled to accept it but they talked to me and I told them that I was sure about my choices. My mum understood but it was very difficult for my dad. I arranged for them to meet Eric but my dad couldn't make eye contact and didn't want to speak. I offered to translate but my dad became very quiet. Gradually he accepted my choice. In the end, I told him Eric had proposed and he was happy for me, but he realised I wouldn't come back to China. It took him more than two years to accept Eric and the relationship. Now my parents have met Eric's parents and have more connection with my new life.

Cassius Lubisi

The first thing I must say is that I am the son of my mother. I was the first graduate in my extended family and I remain the only PhD in my extended family. I am probably an example of what education can do to break the cycle of poverty and cause upward social mobility for individuals and their families. For many people their only inheritance from their parents and grandparents is poverty. Education is a way to break this cycle.

I was born in Nelspruit in eastern South Africa where I went to primary school. In 1980 I left home to go to Inkamana High School in Vryheid, Kwa Zulu Natal. Inkamana was (and still is) a Benedictine school. I was there for five years and we formed a strong community. I still have close contact with the people in the school then and those who followed us. Inkamana is one of the historic church schools which provided quality education during the time of apartheid – a counter-hegemonic school started by the Catholic Church to tackle apartheid from an educational perspective. We had highly qualified teachers who I wouldn't have found in any other Black school at that time.

Looking back this feels like the most important part of my education because there was the freedom to discuss what we were experiencing as black people living under apartheid without being detected by the police. I was in class with the grandson of Chief Albert Luthuli, the first

African to be awarded the Nobel Peace Prize. Chief Luthuli used to provide us with lots of material from the African National Congress (ANC) underground which helped us understand the conditions of apartheid and develop our perspective rather than simply conduct the struggle instinctively.

After high school, I left to join the University of Natal and study for a BSc in mathematics and applied mathematics. After my first year there I was really a part-time student as I had become involved with the underground structures of the then banned ANC. This required me to be away from the university for long stretches of time, sometimes even outside the country. So, the degree ended up taking me seven years. People did not understand why, although the police suspected. The police knew I was an ANC member but did not have the evidence to lock me up. Most of the time I remained one step ahead of them as we had infiltrated the police. We had fellows working for the police who would let us know when they were about to strike. I am probably one of the few anti-apartheid activists who was never arrested; in some instances it was pure luck as the police would arrest everyone at a meeting they thought I was attending but which I had missed and sometimes I avoided the police because I had received information they would be looking for me.

After my extended time at university I took a Higher Diploma in Education which allowed me to become a teacher of mathematics. I had vowed that I would not teach as I would have to work for the apartheid regime. We had defined education as a site of struggle against apartheid. At that time, we had a slogan: 'liberation before education'. We discussed this and arrived at the conclusion that we were being downright stupid to refuse to teach and we changed the slogan to 'education as a site of struggle'. Education became a contested terrain. We appropriated education and turned it into a tool of liberation around 1986, adopting the theories of Freire including the slogan 'pupils' education for pupils' power'. When I received my diploma, I taught mathematics education as well as the social and political aspects of education at the University of Natal.

I should also mention that I briefly taught at the University of Durban in the department of mathematics. There was a big problem there. A very progressive vice-chancellor had been appointed and he started admitting a large number of African students. There were not always systems put in place to support these students and so the pass rate in the first year was only 34 per cent. These students needed scaffolds in place to mediate the mathematics they met at university which they had not met at high school. I went in to set up this system of tutorial support. It was a struggle and there was serious resistance from the old guard who thought that standards were being lowered. They did not want to take instructions from me who was telling them even though they had PhDs in mathematics they were not good teachers. We basically frogmarched the old guard to participate in the programme and in return they made my life hell, to the extent that they made sure that I was not paid for months and months. They thought I would be discouraged but I rocked up every day until I had no resources left. At that point I signalled that this was not working out, these guys have got me, I could not even afford my bus fare to get to the university.

Participating in organisations has also been key in developing my education. University is not only about academic study. University is to educate you in the round. One of my sites of education was the mathematics classroom and the other was the meetings of the ANC student movement. I led the underground education units at university using the university library. Although they had banned all the ANC texts, for some reason they had not banned books written by Lenin and Marx. These became the textbooks in our underground classes.

When I received my diploma, I taught mathematics education as well as the social and political aspects of education at the University of Natal. Then I left for Nottingham in the UK to study for a PhD. Yes, I am a proud Nottingham University Doctoral graduate. I returned home to teach at the University of Natal until I could not resist the pressure, which I had been resisting since 1964, to join government. I had always taken the position that the ANC should be present in all walks of life not just in government positions. During my time at the University of Natal I had been in ministerial task teams with the then Minister of Education, Kader Asmal. He asked me to assist him on a full-time basis as a special adviser.

Later I joined the Department of Education as Deputy Director General responsible for levels Reception to Grade 9. And I was sent to Kwa Zulu Natal to try to sort out the education system there. It was in a total mess. They turned to me and said can you come and help us here; we have to take this thing out of the mud as soon as possible. So, I went there to try and turn things round. It was difficult but we did turn it round in a very short period of time. The department had previously been ruled as a dictatorship; we democratised the department, everyone could make suggestions. We ran the department under collective respon-sibility with collective decision making. We built new schools, we built sanitation facilities, we provided computers and science laboratories. I am really proud of that period and my role in turning the department around. I was then approached by President Zuma to come to the presidency. I am now Director General and Secretary to the Cabinet. It is a job at the apex of public service in South Africa.

My view has always been to be at the service of the people. If I can contribute to improving the lives of others then I will accept the chal-lenge. Of course, during the struggle that meant liberating the people and now it means improving the lives of the people using the state machinery.

Haana Sandy

I am an Iranian woman who grew up in a family in which education was, and continues to be, highly valued. My mum's side of the family has a hunger for learning, and teaching has been in her family's blood for centuries. My mum is a big influence in my life, but she never asked me to be a teacher or even study mathematics. She encourages me all the time to never stop learning and exploring; she doesn't rec-ognise failure. My heritage from my mum is to 'never stop trying' which was her motto. I must also acknowledge my father's contribu-tion to my life. Even though my father is not highly educated he was supportive of me going to university and was happy to pay for it. My father is calm and respectful to people; for him education is about learning to be tolerant.

When I was a teenager I had lots of questions about so many of the things I was surrounded by: in particular religion and some of the cul-tural restrictions in my country. I attempted to satisfy my curiosity draw-ing on my family and relatives, and then broadened my sources to well-known people who claimed to have answers. I read many texts but never found the answers. I was convinced that I could not believe many of the things that I was told as they simply did not make sense to me. Always there seemed to be too many 'red lines' which I was told not to cross.

Looking back, it feels like I was mostly self-educated. At school, I thought, 'I'm not going to learn anything here; I'll go home and study'. I found the whole of my education boring. In Iranian schools neither pupils nor teachers are encouraged or trained to be tolerant about other views or cultures.

I studied for my degree in Iran in a different city from the one I was born and grew up in. I loved studying to become a teacher. Teaching is seen as a respectable profession and is seen as especially good for women. When I became a teacher, I worked really hard during the day but was home by two-o'clock and able to enjoy having dignity, time and independence at the same time. In my first year of teaching on an annual 'Teacher Day' I was nominated by the head teacher as a successful, dedicated and hard-working teacher. However, my name was never announced at the ceremony. The day after, I was told it was because 'you are advocating alternative ways of thinking' and my work uniform was not loose enough. I was not wearing a full hijab in the way defined by the state.

Unfortunately, conditions in Iran meant that I was forced to leave my homeland. It was a big decision and risky but I made it to England. It has been tough, so tough. When I arrived in the UK I volunteered in a number of places at the same time and studied English, IT skills and numeracy to become familiar with the basic language and concepts of mathematics in English. Then I accepted a taster experience in a secondary school. I was really happy to get that experience. I thought, 'I am a teacher. I will teach in a school like this'. The atmosphere was warm and inviting, so different from any school in Iran where schools feel more formal and unwelcoming. While coming to understand the huge differences between schools in the UK and those that I had become used to in Iran I became violently sick with terrible headaches for days. I wondered how I could face all the challenges at the same time. Then I thought, 'shall I sit back and be on the margins all my life, or shall I take control?' Finding the way into teaching here was like opening a gate in a very thick wall. It was the first step. It is difficult to explain but I had been frozen by everything around me, I was in my shell, everything was abstract, I was existing in two different worlds.

I am now a secondary mathematics teacher in Leeds and teach mathematics in English, which is my third language. My mother tongue is Kurdish, but I studied throughout my education in Farsi, the official language of Iran. I never gave up on my dream of becoming a teacher again when I arrived in Leeds. Living and working in my third language was and remains difficult. I am away from the comfort zone of my motherland where most things are easier to manage, apart from having very few human rights. It was so difficult to decide to come here, a mixture of joy and pain for me, sometimes I wish I had not come. I have experienced and gone through so much. I know I can manage my life here but having to continuously communicate in a language that I have not grown up with is very tiring; when I speak my own language, it is effortless.

I wouldn't have thought that I could have coped with so many challenges in my work and life. In some ways they have made me stronger. But emotionally I sometimes feel delicate here. I'm thinking in two or even three languages constantly, sometimes I have to translate mathematics or a problem into Kurdish or Farsi then English. I find handling two cultures tiring, it is a difficult situation, but here I feel like my skin has thinned. It is not because I have become weaker, but I think it is because I have had to be so strong for too long. I make sure that I get out on long walks, escaping into nature makes me strong again. I continue to make sure I know what is going on around the world and remain aware of the changes we are going through as human beings.

I think it is beyond most of my colleagues' comprehension to know what it would be like to work in a totally different system and in a different language, so I hope for more understanding from them. I hope my students, especially those who have been forced to be displaced or those with horrific family stories will have opportunities to flourish and reach their full potential just like other students. I hope they gain what they deserve while enjoying their childhood.

Helen Toft

I am a 60-year-old woman, how old that seems, and very much a family woman. I'm a mother, granny, wife and carer. I include the Labour party as 'family' and enjoy nurturing that sense within the local branch. Thinking about it, I often try to create a sense of family in all that I do, maybe because my own family was disrupted.

Initially I was a classroom teacher but I'm not that any more. This feels simultaneously like a long time ago and yet still fresh. For example a recent experience of teaching first-year undergraduate students did remind me of the excitement of my time in the classroom. I describe myself now as a teacher trainer in an international/online context. Until I went to university to study English I never really saw teaching as one of the 'caring' professions but after graduation I made the connections between teaching and nursing or social work. I still wonder if I would have made a good social worker as that connects closely with the political slant that I have on teaching.

I loved my third year at university because I was expected to dig deep into one area of literature and focus on a single author. It made me want to stay on at university and I couldn't think of anything apart from studying to become a teacher. I had two wonderful teachers when I was at school and I think they inspired me to become a teacher. They were both teachers of English. One was a man I was really scared of but who knew about literature and the other was a young woman who always did exciting things with us including drama. She also came from the North of England, which was where I saw home to be. She was a very special teacher who was also really approachable. Her dad ran a sweet shop in Glossop which seemed ordinary to me and so I think she made teaching seem like something I could do. As we have aged I have realised that my dad had a big influence on me but that I was always kicking against this influence because he left my mum, my brother and me when I was 8 years old. He has recently started talking about his history and I wonder if the value I place on education has been largely influenced by him. His family were all involved in political education: trade union training; the Workers Education Association and so on, while my mum has always been cautious of higher education. She saw me as having aspirations which were above myself if I did things like read a book and was more comfortable with me doing ironing or housework above homework.

The most important part of my teaching career was when I spent a year on secondment from school working with colleagues at Sheffield University to redesign the whole curriculum for the school I was teaching in. We were expected to be reflective and to keep commonplace books. This was a time when I was a part of a team and it was the team that was the most important thing for me. This is also where my interest in cross-curricular work first blossomed.

I enjoy encouraging political discussions within my local community which feels a bit like my classroom. I am convinced these sessions make a difference within the community and people seem eager for the next one; many value the chance to learn about something new. Similarly, I am involved in a cross-generational choir, another 'family', where older people are challenged to learn something new and develop new skills. This has been inspirational for me. I've been acting as a teaching assistant to Nik who is running the choir, a 'teacher' at the beginning of his career.

The international dimension to my work has always been rooted in my own classroom. For example, right from the beginning I was determined to teach multicultural literature to the learners in the outskirts of Rotherham and Sheffield, even though they kicked against it and couldn't/wouldn't see the point. I had been amazed that such a thing as African literature existed when I was introduced to it at university. When our children were growing up we lived in Leicester. Here my multicultural beliefs became solidly anti-racist as we were living in an amazingly multicultural town and my daughter was in a predominantly Asian school. Later I was involved in a Europe-wide project looking at inclusive education in Denmark, Spain and the UK. I now find it very strange if I am working in a room which does not have an internationalist perspective.

This also comes from my drama association with the National Association of Teaching through Drama (NATD) which always sees an international perspective. I worked with the NATD in Bosnia just after the war and this was another incredible experience. The conference we ran asked the question, 'How do you educate young people when two years ago they were surrounded by killing, even killing each other?' I was suddenly very humbled and nervous: would I be able to offer anything? It ended up being totally transformative and I am still very close to the people I was working with. I have carried out all of this while overcoming my fear of travel, I am literally travel sick. I have come a long way from a background in which I was not expected to lead or 'make my mark' at all.

I always love the way people I work with surprise me and in turn I want to collaborate and inspire them to change something; ultimately, I want children and young people to have amazing experiences which will change their lives. I know this is possible because that is what education did for me.

Jarret Voytilla

I'm known as J. I'm 40 years old and Canadian by birth. I spent the first 27 years of my life in Canada, then I left and I haven't been back since except for a few months here and there.

I started studying forestry at the University of Alberta, but quickly changed to physics. After two years of that, I realised it was not a good fit for me and took a two-year hiatus to reconsider my goals and direction.

When I returned to university, I focused on anthropology and biology. After a year, biology won out and I completed my BSc the following year. During my final semester I had three jobs, two part-time and one full-time. I was getting tired of working all the time, and envious of my friends who were going off on gap years. I thought, 'I so wish I could do that', as I was getting sick of doing nothing but studying and working crap jobs. So, I thought, 'well what's this teaching English in Korea thing about?' and started looking into it.

To be honest, I always thought that teaching was the most depressing job I could ever imagine having. I remember thinking in high school, 'this is one thing I'm not doing'. Because you just stand there in the same place while people pass you by, moving up and beyond your horizon, like you're on an island watching the party drift by you on boats, waving at you. However, I told myself that this is the teaching English avenue, not real teaching. It will get me to travel, and then I'll come back and do my Masters.

We had a jobcentre on campus and I started looking at all these different jobs advertised in Korea. One of my friends said she'd seen a job advertised in Mexico. She knew I was studying Spanish and I was dating a Latino girl so she thought I might be interested. It wasn't teaching English, it was teaching science, and considering I'd studied pretty much everything in science, I thought, 'Wow I could be pretty good at this'. So, I applied for it, got an interview, and somehow the recruiter believed that I knew what I was doing in my mock class presentation and hired me.

The company I joined was a massive, private Mexican institution. I was part of a group of 15 foreigners whose job was to teach our respective subject areas, but in English. They piled us all together and ran us through some training, my first real teacher training. When I got to my campus I fell under the wing of my department head and another lady who was a senior biology teacher, and between the two of them they pretty much shaped me into an effective and professional educator, who was in control and not just responding to things that happened in the classroom. Arturo and Rebeca were my first mentors, and they raised me. One year of escape became seven, and the start of a new and unexpected career. It's hard to reflect on it now but it seems that this was my first time of being in a place where the community had a different perspective. Learning to exist in a society where you just don't fit in anywhere was good training for me. Nothing you ever do as an outsider is ever going to change anything in the system you're in. Real change happens from within a society. All you can do is help people make that change. You can't be that change.

I became more involved in my professional development as years rolled by. I got a seat on the Academia, our educational senate, and when we started incorporating the IB programme onto our campus, I got my first IB training and started teaching IB classes. I also became a teacher trainer, a trainer of other schools' teachers and our own. Then I felt I plateaued. I thought maybe it's time to go back to Canada and do that Masters. I moved back, and started looking into funding and research grants. I volunteered for a while and looked around for jobs. I had it in my head that what I wanted to do was public health but I had to wait another year to apply because I missed the deadline. To fill the gap I got involved with Cuso International, a scheme we have in Canada which is similar to Voluntary Service Overseas (VSO) in the UK, and I got involved with them. They had a position in Ghana as an institutional consultant or something and were vague on the details, which was exciting. They did ask me if I could ride a motorbike from village to village though, which was a little scary. I was asked to train local teachers and to get more girls into school.

Then one morning, in late August 2011, I was perusing educational job-sites just for fun and there was a job advertised for a science teacher at a travelling school. I couldn't believe my eyes. I immediately applied and was hired. Six years later I have now diversified myself into teaching both science and humanities courses, as well as become a bit of an expert on travel, experiential learning and curriculum design. The founder of the Global school changed my life. The organisation she has created and the people that she hired to run it are close friends of mine now. They have given me opportunity, challenged me, and pushed me way beyond where I thought my comfort zone ended. I now see no limits to what education can look like, or how it can transform.

I learned how to adjust myself and adjust my own perspectives. Now I live in Thailand when I am not travelling for work and that's another society where I am an outsider. However, after being globally adrift for 15 years, this feels normal. It is quite liberating really. You can join the local society, but you do not get judged on the same terms for your successes or lack thereof. You see reality. If someone is poor and begging on the street you see that right in front of you, not buried off across the tracks behind a wall somewhere. It feels more honest and helps me to never forget that there are issues to work on and to be thankful for the luck I have had in my life. I guess what travelling has done aside from make me happy is to realise that you don't need to travel so much to see humans being humans, because basically we're the same everywhere.

I hope that the students I work with don't walk away from this school and just become an accountant somewhere. If they are going to be an accountant I hope they work for a non-governmental organisation (NGO) that their friend is establishing and that that NGO is going to be the next Amnesty International. I hope they participate in the world around them in a meaningful way and try to make changes. This is about strength of character. Integrity. I don't want my students to be influenced by the herd because they'll want them to conform because it's easier. I hope they feel strong enough to go back to their own community or to find new communities and that they inspire people.

Reflections

We believe that our own autobiographies play a role in the sorts of teachers we become. As we started the process of writing this book we were interested to discover how our autobiographies would intersect and in what ways they would differ. We tried not to influence each other's writing too much and so while we all started from the same series of questions we did not share early drafts of our writing.

As we reread the autobiographies we felt as though some common stories, common memories came through. In their different ways, our families and friends have had a very close influence on our development as educators, either in supporting us in our learning or in influencing us in important life choices. We can also see many instances of our parents valuing education in its broadest sense although for some there was a cultural clash in terms of education being seen as something for people other than 'us'. For those of us not directly supported by parents or who were in some senses excluded from formal education, education was our way to escape.

Many of the stories show the authors as fiercely determined to continue with education as lifelong learners despite the many challenges that life or the education system in which we grew up threw at us. We became skilled at finding our own ways to learn if we were not inspired or enthused by the official curriculum. Indeed, the autobiographies suggest that many of us were bored by the formal curriculum offered at school or university. For some this resulted in a refusal to do things that clash with deeply held values and beliefs even though that may cause us difficulties.

Many of us found ways to learn outside formal settings. Often this took the form of reading widely. We found authors that excited us and that connected with our values and beliefs, or that took us outside our current situation, and we read avidly. There is a sense of liberation and freedom through reading in several of our stories. We also felt that the author team seemed to see the positive even in the most difficult circumstances. There is the sense of looking for the next opportunity rather than dwelling on past difficulties.

It might be unsurprising that in an author team exploring global education we share a sense that travel is an important part of our lives and education. Some of us are deliberate travellers and some fell upon travelling by accident. For some travel came from feeling held back by the 'local' and jumping at opportunities that presented themselves. Several stories tell of having the courage to take risks, of needing excitement and challenge. This has led to us taking advantage of the serendipitous opportunity. As well as valuing travel, we acknowledge the sense of culture shock that comes through moving and living in different cultures. There is also an acknowledgement that working in different languages and across cultures can offer freedom but is also very challenging and often far from comfortable.

Finally, there is a sense that care and love are an important part of teaching for us all. We all share an emotional attachment to our stories of learning and realise that learning only takes place in an atmosphere of trust and love. We learn best from someone who cares about us and who we care about.

Figure 3.1 Graphical summary: Who are we?

Commonplace book: Entry 3

We would like you to follow the same process as the author team in researching your personal starting point. After asking the question 'who are you?' over and over we had to allow for long silences to allow us to dredge up all the different roles we play in and out of our roles as educators. Try the same activity. As many times as you can, answer the question

Who are you?

Who are you?

Who are you?

Who are you?

Who are you?

Follow this up by writing about your most vivid memory of your own schooling. Write it in as much detail as possible. If you feel confident, talk about it with a friend or a colleague. This will help you remember the detail. Then try to answer these questions in about 200 words each. This will form the next section of your commonplace book.

What has influenced your direction in life?

What were the most meaningful parts of your education?

How did education fit in with the values held at home?

What are the international dimensions of your life?

What are your hopes for those that you work with?

Part 2

Our experiences as learners

Chapter 4

My day in education

We realised early in the process of education that while most of us still describe ourselves as educators we all spend our days very differently. The diverse ways in which we engage in education and educating, on a daily basis, are appropriate symbols for the diverse ways in which we all learn and the many different facets that teaching or educating can take.

We hope that the glimpses of our day-to-day lives that follow resonate with you and maybe offer a glimpse of the way that things could be in the future. Teachers walk down many different paths after that first tentative step into becoming a teacher.

Lucy Cooker

In the UK – working on campus

I get up at 6am, have tea and breakfast, and then drive to campus, which takes an hour and ten minutes. I swim 30 lengths of the pool before I start work. As all my teaching is online, the bulk of that work involves logging on to our virtual learning environment (VLE) to mark students' assignments and provide feedback on written work, meeting students on Skype for tutorials and providing support via email. My work also includes thinking, reading and writing (for example, today I was writing an article based on work done for a research project looking at social and emotional wellbeing in international schools); supervising doctoral students and attending meetings. Sometimes I go and work in the Starbucks on campus for a change of scene and sometimes we hold meetings in the university café, Aspire. I usually bring leftovers for my lunch. I leave work around 4.45pm and drive home, arriving around 6.15pm.

Usually, my partner Claire will have cooked dinner, and we eat together. I will continue working in the evening, and go to bed around 11pm.

In the UK – working at home

I get up at 6am, make tea, and then Claire and I take our dog, Flo, out for a 40-minute walk. When we get home, I have breakfast, shower and then get down to work around 8.30am. When I work from home I try to prioritise writing and other tasks for which I need no interruptions and a long period of concentration. I might draft, refine or edit an article, draft a book proposal, review a journal article, or write a report; or I may read and comment on draft chapters of theses or mark challenging pieces of work submitted by students. I have occasional breaks when I make tea and play with Flo. I eat lunch sitting at my desk. I stop work at 5.30pm and take Flo for another walk. On days when I work at home I usually cook dinner, or we might go to our local pub for pizza and then I will continue working in the evening, usually going to bed around 11pm.

Not in the UK – teaching

I spend up to five weeks every year away from home teaching the PGCEi face-to-face induction sessions in our overseas hubs. These teaching sessions have taken me mostly to Bangkok and Kuala Lumpur (KL), but also to Singapore, Ghana (and Nottingham). I also travel to set up new cohorts and to inspect the teaching venue and facilities and to ensure they meet the required university standards. When I'm in Bangkok and KL, I stay in a hotel with my colleagues who also teach as part of the same team. I get up at 6am and join my colleagues for breakfast at 7am. Over breakfast we may discuss the teaching we have planned for the day. We start teaching at 8.30am. Our teaching days are intense; we will break for lunch in the middle of the day and have a couple of tea breaks, but otherwise teach until 4.30 or 5pm. I will then return to my room and may have a quick swim in the hotel pool, but always spend a little time catching up on emails which have started to come in as my UK colleagues are just starting work. I will join my colleagues for drinks at 6.30 and dinner a little later. I will return to my room around 10pm and usually have a chat with Claire on FaceTime before continuing with work, marking, emailing, or Skyping with students/colleagues until 1 or 2am.

Not in the UK – research

I may spend up to seven weeks a year travelling for research. Usually on these trips I'm visiting international schools to interview students, teachers and parents. In the last three years I have visited schools in Thailand, China, Indonesia, Spain, Peru, USA, Kenya, Singapore, the United Arab Emirates (UAE) and the UK. On these visits I may stay at the school or in a nearby hotel. I'm usually up by 6am, catching up on emails and marking before breakfast, and then travel to the school for the start of the day. It is normal to spend a whole day in school, getting a feel for the institution and meeting with a variety of different research participants. Sometimes there are evening events which I also need to attend, but otherwise I will have dinner at school or close to my hotel, before returning to my room to FaceTime Claire, and then work on emails, marking and writing until the early hours of the morning.

Tony Cotton

It is very hard to think of a day that is typical for me so I shall describe what I am doing today, Sunday 30 October 2016. Yes, I sometimes work on a Sunday. But if you are a teacher and reading this you know all about that. The joy for me is that on this particular Sunday I am working in Bangkok teaching on the PGCEi that inspired us to write this book. I am lucky enough to work around the world on interesting projects. I am also lucky enough, or maybe just old enough, to be asked to work on these projects rather than to have to write bids or apply for the work.

So, as I write, I am sitting outside the teaching room making the most of the time when I am not teaching. I have just completed the first proofs for edition 254 of *Mathematics Teaching*. I am currently the editor of this journal which is sent free to all members of the Association of Teachers of Mathematics. As a part of this role I publish a blog every Monday morning. My blog this week referred to the PGCEi course and the joy of working with a diverse range of participants. As I wrote on the blog,

> The joy of working with such a diverse group is that there are no assumptions as to the way that things should be. When the shared experience of being taught is so diverse the knowledge we have to draw on offers us many possibilities. So, for much of today I will be working with this wonderful group, sharing ideas with them to set them off on their year long journey of distance learning.

But there are other tasks that I need to work on today. Other tasks that pop up in my calendar to remind me that I have what I believe is called, a portfolio career. The course in Bangkok finishes tomorrow. The day after that I fly to Singapore for a meeting with a UK publisher and the publishers of a Singapore mathematics programme. Currently there is global interest in the approach adopted in Singaporean schools to teaching mathematics. As with any programme there are things that we can all learn from and things that we may want to critique. But I have been asked by the publisher to work with local writers to adapt a programme for international schools around the world. Today I have to come up with some sample material. Looking at my calendar I will be putting this together between 5.00 and 6.30 this evening.

The other task I need to work on today is another writing project. I have been asked to write a mathematics programme for primary schools in Jamaica. The Jamaican government have just introduced a new standards curriculum and have put the call out for publishers to tender for books which they will buy for all schools on the island. I visited Jamaica two weeks ago for the initial research and development workshops and meetings. I met teachers and visited schools to create a plan for the programme. It now must be written before my next visit when we will share it with the teachers for their comment and critique. This allows us to make any changes before the books are submitted to the government. So, I had better get on with Unit 2, 'Measurement: Focus question: what units should I use to measure things in my environment?'

Edward Emmett

Every work day starts the same. I wake up at 7am, ride my scooter to school avoiding potholes, fallen cables and extreme weather wherever possible. When I arrive and pass the security guards on the gate I arrive in our lovely school grounds which are really beautiful. The buildings in school are growing rapidly. Six years ago we only had six classes with children aged 2–8 years old. We now have 21 classes aged between 2 and 14 years old. I have witnessed a lot of change and the school now has four playgrounds, a swimming pool, science labs under construction as well as grass and all-weather football pitches. I am responsible for seven early years classes in three different buildings as I am the early years' coordinator. All the classrooms are air conditioned and have projector screens but not interactive whiteboards. Teaching starts at 9am when most of the children and my two Thai assistants arrive. Some are later but I try to get them to come on time because at 9.20 we start the 'Songs of Sound' scheme with flashcards, games and songs. Then we move onto literacy or our theme lesson for the term.

Snack time is at 10.15. I encourage fruit but some children bring chocolate or candy; however, we have a 'Fresh Fruit Friday' where on that day only fruit is allowed. Playtime is outside in an average of 28° under canopies and I am free to plan, write up observations or conduct meetings while my class go to Thai, music, PE, art, Chinese and computers until lunchtime. We have a shop, smoothie bar and canteen serving quail egg soup, dim sum, chicken and rice, western style food and sandwiches. During lunch playtime there are clubs and activities to attend and I coach girls' football.

My lesson observations are given in to the office every Friday, which sends them to the government. Although I think no one looks at them, they help me develop my teaching and understanding. We used to be a full Montessori school, but now, because the owner still likes the method but wants to move over to the English framework, we only teach in this style for 30 minutes a day when it should be a session of three hours minimum.

At 1.30pm our mathematics lessons begin; we follow a UK programme but we learn through play, beginning to use whiteboards to work together and draw answers. By 2.10pm we are reading stories or playing games on the mat ready for the end of school or after school clubs till 4pm. The clubs include English, swimming, art, clay, Thai and Chinese and parents can request a teacher to stay till 4pm for a parent consultation.

My Thai assistants and I have a chat and leave about 4.15pm. I have worked well for four years with one of my assistants who I could not teach without. My other assistant doesn't speak much English but tries her best, although it is mainly an English-speaking Thai class, with a few Koreans where children translate for us until English is learned in around four months, with fluency achieved in a year. I don't really take work home except for reports once a term. The only marking I have is literacy which I tend to finish in school. So, I have a lot of free time and holidays. I am not paid the top teacher's salary but then I have a much more relaxed time than those under pressure in the top international schools. Mine is a school led by an owner who is a bit of a local hero. The owner espouses a 'family atmosphere' and most jobs are given to those connected to the school even if they are not qualified; but even here the pressure is beginning to develop. Most children will stay on in our school for their primary education because the curriculum is popular, but some will transfer to a top-flight secondary school to continue their education.

Lisa Fernandes

I started my career as a teaching assistant just over two years ago in Bangalore in an international school which follows the IB programme. This year I am wearing two hats. I work in the learning support department for two days a week and for the other three days I co-teach in Grade 5, as I am being mentored to become a homeroom teacher next year. I am also the cover teacher for when teachers go on extended leave. This enables continuity for the students and has given me a wonderful opportunity to experience my own class for an extended period and to plan lessons across the primary school. When I arrive each morning, I don't know which hat I will be wearing. I am enjoying the learning and the experience I am getting with each class. I feel I am appreciated for being flexible and enthusiastic whether I am teaching Grade 1 or Grade 6 pupils, art, music or PE.

I have about a 1-hour commute to our beautiful school far from the city's smog and dust. I leave home at 6.30am and my school day starts at 7.25am. On a regular week, I go straight to my Grade 6 class. Children in this grade are 10–11 years old and independent. There is a gradual transfer of responsibility from teachers to pupils this year as they prepare for middle school next year. With an increased emphasis this year on technology in education in our school most of the lessons are posted on Google Classroom. The school provides an iPad for every child in the primary years' programme on which the pupils access their mathematics, language or unit of inquiry activities. They also submit their work online. Every day we have an hour each of mathematics, language and 'unit of inquiry' with an additional three specialist classes of music, art and PE and an additional languages session. Classes start at 7.50am. We have two blocks in the morning ending at 9.45am with a snack break for 20 minutes. Then back to class for two more blocks with collaborative planning time, when the students go to their specialist classes, ending with a lunch break from 12 to 1pm. Most of the students and teachers eat school food, cooked on the premises, in a big airy cafeteria. We have a choice of Indian or continental food. I normally have either a playground monitoring duty or choir rehearsal or some practice or another to attend from 12.30 to 1pm. After lunch we have one teaching block, ending in another

20-minute break, followed by the last block for the students till the end of school at 3pm. On Tuesdays and Thursdays my day ends at 4pm after an extra curricula activity (ECA). Each teacher has to offer an ECA either on a Tuesday or a Thursday. I take the children's choir with another teacher. The choir sings at the winter concert and the year-end concert. On Mondays and Wednesdays we have staff meetings meaning I get home by about 5.45.

It is a long day especially for those students who face a long commute. I am trying to make the most of this year by observing other teachers and adding to my toolbox of strategies to prepare for a homeroom position next year. I reach home exhausted but deeply satisfied, as I am doing what I love doing in a truly international school that is very well resourced with highly experienced practitioners.

Han Wei

I currently work in a small, not-for-profit language school, teaching Chinese. I have nine students, as my classroom is small so I can only seat nine. They have progressed to Year 1 from Pinyin class which is the class for students designed to learn the Chinese pronunciation system. Three of my students are English-born Chinese; three are English–Chinese, one is English–African, and two are British-born Spanish. Only one of them has Chinese as their mother tongue. They are aged from 7 to 10 years old, plus one 12-year-old student and one 14-year-old student. They all have English names and some of them have Chinese names. Recently I've given the other students a Chinese name and there are various reasons for this. First, it helps to create more of a Chinese culture in the class. Also, it helps the students to practise pronunciations and listening through calling their names.

On each Sunday morning, I wake up between 8 and 9 to design my lessons. I generally have breakfast first. Sometimes I have noodles and sometimes I have cereal, toast or porridge. I do my lesson planning at home. Planning my lessons takes me less time than it used to. It used to take me about four hours, but now I have more experience and a fairly useful book, so it takes less time. Previously I didn't have any resources, because the school is a non-profit organisation and there weren't many suitable materials for my class, so I had to design everything from scratch, including the syllabus.

I have some frustrations with the textbook as it is based on a grammar-translation based teaching method and is not up-to-date, but I'm required to use it. I like to make my lesson more fun and interactive, so consequently I use the lesson plans and some activities from the book, and supplement those with my own ideas.

When I've finished planning my lessons I'll have a cup of tea and a bite of lunch – usually noodles or rice – before I go to work. My classes start at 12.15. The first half of the lesson is for one hour followed by a 15-minute break, then we have the second half for 45 minutes. Generally, for the first session, we have 10–20 minutes' review, and then I'll teach the new content. I give some input and then allow them to practise. They have time to learn vocabulary, practise sentence structure, and listening. So before the break it's mostly speaking and listening, and after the break it's writing and more activities. It's usually easier for the students to concentrate in the second session. Recently we've been learning about each other and we've been learning about our names by playing a game that is typically used to learn names in China.

The head teacher of the school encourages everyone to practise typing. They type sentences or characters on their phones or tablets. During break we practise typing exercises in Chinese. In English you type the letter, but in Chinese you type the letter and the software changes it to Chinese characters. You need to recognise the correct character and select it. The use of computers makes the writing of Chinese much easier as you don't need to remember the order of the strokes. This makes the use of writing much more likely. There are so many similar characters in Chinese, so the problem with typing is that it makes the different characters harder to recognise. Therefore, writing remains important, especially for understanding the formation and meaning of the characters; but typing does have advantages and helps students recognise characters.

After 45 minutes I give homework to the students. I used to print off the homework, and ask them to stick it in their homework diary, but now they are one year older so they can copy it down. Then the lesson finishes.

I return all the materials and clear up and sometimes I need to talk to the head about various issues, for example, related to classroom management, and then she might give me some advice. After the lesson I also meet the parents who are there to pick up their children and advise them about how to guide their students' learning at home.

My husband, Eric, always comes to pick me up after school and asks me how the class went. We talk about the class and I tell him about the students who have progressed well. He sometimes has some good ideas about what to do in the class. He gives me feedback about my teaching. Sometimes, when I'm feeling lazy, Eric pushes me to make me reflect more deeply on my teaching and to help me be a better teacher.

Sometimes we go to the Chinese supermarket close to the school, to get Chinese ingredients, and then we go home and cook. In the evening we sometimes go out for a walk or go shopping, or sometimes just relax at home.

Cassius Lubisi

There is no such thing as a typical day. Things get very hectic here. I spend most of my days in meetings which can be very debilitating as it takes you away from direct contact with the people. I tend to wake up about 4.45am as I need to do some walking to be refreshed and this is the only time I can do this. It clears my mind and I find it is a good time for thinking. This has always been the case. I remember I did my best theoretical work for my PhD in Nottingham when I was out running in the mornings.

If I'm in Pretoria I will then go to the Union buildings, the seat of government. If I'm in Cape Town I go to De Tuynhuys, the presidential offices, and start with a briefing from my PAs who remind me of what is in my diary and what I am doing in the day. Things change; some envoy might have come in from Chad and the president needs supporting or I may need to go to support a minister of state.

On Tuesdays and Wednesdays I sit in cabinet committees which process cabinet work and take recommendations to full cabinet the following week. In full cabinet, I am locked in the meeting as I am the final arbiter of the cabinet decisions and have to rule on these. I also advise the president during the meetings.

On some days I call meetings of specific task teams which I chair. For example, I chair the task team on migration. In April 2015 there were instances of xenophobic attacks in three townships and the president set up this task group to ensure we assist with the matter permanently. Migration is a big thing in South Africa as it is in the European Union (EU) and the United States. We receive more migrants into South Africa than the whole of the EU combined. All sub-Saharan migrants come here. We have a very progressive policy, we don't do camps, and people can go anywhere they want. Sometimes I will receive a note from one of the townships warning me that trouble is brewing so I will deploy people to go and find out what is happening to try and resolve the tensions.

I also call myself the South African Government undertaker. If there is a death which requires a state funeral I convene meetings to put this together. I also chair the task team on the reform of state-owned companies, and I will call and chair meetings with state-owned companies to call them to account.

On some days, we do go to the people to see what is happening. I will travel with the president and we directly engage with communities to find out what their needs are, what their complaints with government are. We try to give them answers on the spot. We see direct contact as vital for our government to make sure we do not lose touch with our people.

Sometimes I have one-on-one meetings with the president and deputy president to bounce ideas off each other; sometimes I meet diplomats with the president. I am also the Chancellor of National Orders – this means I am responsible for running the system of selecting people who receive honours.

The earliest time I will ever get to bed is 11pm but it is often up to 2.30am. When President Mandela died we went three days without sleeping. We said goodbye to the sun and then hello again the next morning without sleeping. This can also happen during times of inauguration of new presidents. That is probably my toughest job. The transition to the next government in 2019 will probably be the last time I do this before I return to the academy.

Haana Sandy

I wake at 6.30am, dress smartly and have breakfast before driving 30 minutes or so to work listening to music or the news on the radio. I take my lesson plans from my laptop and print them out. There is often a long queue for the photocopier, but I take the relevant sheets and presentation slides and any other equipment in my trolley to each of my many teaching classrooms.

Form time (Homeroom) is at 8.45am and has a set routine of checking homework and stamping pupil's planners to show that I have checked them. I talk to students and challenge any poor behaviour, spend time building relationships and I feel I am very successful in this aspect of my role. At first the boys tended to be very arrogant, but now they are friendly when I ask them about their day. The more organised I am for lessons the better I can deal with the behaviour of some students. My first lesson is with the highest attaining 15–16-year-old students which I really enjoy. I have to refresh my knowledge constantly to work with this group and the post-16 statistics group. This means that I have to make sure I have answered all the questions myself before I ask the students to work on them. I enjoy the challenge of such new territory. Sometimes even these groups can shock me with the gaps in their knowledge and I have to go back over material that I had expected them to be familiar with.

Later in the day I have a group of lower-attaining students which I also enjoy. I've had a good experience this year. There were some immature boys who were always seeking compliments, but they are responding to my teaching. Other teachers said, 'Oh, good luck with "that lot"' I had a girl who was really challenging but I put her on report and now she calls me 'your majesty' as a joke. I find at first they might be defensive because they fear they won't understand my questions, but they know now I genuinely care and will support them. There is even a 15-year-old boy whose literacy level was equivalent to a seven-year-old and he is talking and joining in now.

Whenever I take over a new class they complain about my accent. They don't like difference, and it makes them think I am not a good teacher. They 'act up' and give me a hard time. This is very hard and can be frustrating but I am patient and once we build a good relationship this phase passes.

There are 20-minute breaks between lessons but this is not my own time. I spend the time setting up a classroom or printing materials, or talking to a student. At most I might catch five minutes for a drink and a piece of fruit.

I take my own lunch box and catch up with work while I eat. We have a small faculty office to use for work, and the staff room has a fridge, microwave, water. You hardly ever see mathematics or science teachers in the shared staffroom. We always have something to do and our office is a friendly place to be.

The bell for the end of the school day goes at 3pm but I don't stop work then. Every Monday there is a staff or department meeting. The rest of the week after school clubs is mostly revision for final examinations and a mathematics department 'detention' once a week which two staff run together. I am a special educational needs (SEND) champion and I also have responsibility for the more able. I have also been asked to volunteer as an English as an Additional Language (EAL) teacher and have taken on a Kurdish Syrian student this year for one hour a week.

After meetings I will call parents if their child has been disruptive or very good at something. Sometimes the parents are very defensive if you are saying their child is being challenging. There is so much bureaucracy and paperwork for a teacher that it is a real burden. I catch up with marking and usually leave school about 6.30pm. My day is very draining. The thing I don't like about the system in the UK is a tendency to 'spoon feed' and blame the teacher for everything. It is a very complex thing, to do with society and culture; but there is too much pressure on teachers and children here and the children have not been taught to learn independently. This can all lead to not getting good results in tests and exams. It may be a controversial thing to say but the system needs changing. I have a friend who teaches in Canada where it is very difficult to become a teacher, but once there the 'blame' is not on the teacher.

Evenings are a meal, working on my laptop, sometimes catching up with Facebook news about the Middle East, thinking about Iran and Syria. If I'm lucky I will have time to watch 'The Great British Bake Off' or a comedy, and I call home once a week. If I won the lottery I would still want to teach, but not like this. With no free time the system will be in crisis, the workload is so huge a human body cannot keep up under the pressure. It is such a contrast to Iran where the government is so corrupt and does not really want children to be educated and think for themselves, so there is little organisation or structure. I am not saying the UK should be like that but we are working 50–70 hours a week and that is not healthy either.

Helen Toft

I have chosen one particular day of the week to describe, a Thursday. Every day of my week is different since I retired from teaching and lecturing, when, of course, I had similar timetable demands as any teacher around the world. This new-found freedom is both exciting and demanding. Because I now teach an online university course I can choose to tutor or mark students' work at any time of day or night. But other responsibilities and commitments mean that I do have some fixed points in the week, and Thursdays are a good example of this. My online tutoring is my overt teaching but the other ways I spend my day are intimately involved in my own and others' lifelong learning.

Thursdays begin with ringing my elderly mum to check she's OK and remind her that it is choir today. I have had to learn a lot very quickly about supporting someone with severe memory loss especially as her confusion about day-to-day activities causes her a great deal of anxiety. Singing together in an intergenerational choir has offered us both a lifeline, an anchor of calm in her week; that means Thursdays tend to begin on a more positive note.

After the phone call I check university emails which will include administration, questions and discussion. Sometimes students have serious challenges and upsets in their lives, meaning they need a little more support. I also check messages and Facebook posts from an organisation I chair. Attempting to bring the sort of social justice I promote in education to the community of the market town in which I live is absorbing, demanding and frustrating in equal measure.

Next I meet the choir leader for coffee. Local coffee shops replace staffrooms and departmental offices when you retire. Nik, the choir leader, is a great teacher, a young friend and a political ally, so as well as planning for the choir session we discuss the latest political developments and share ideas for change in our shared world. The community I live in can be rather suspicious of newcomers and, as Nik was standing to represent the town in local council elections he needed to become better known. Using his music skills was an obvious way to make a connection with older people in our town. I was to be his teaching assistant as well as organising the room that we were to meet in.

Learning in a group of 30 people with an average age in the late 70s has been a revelation for me. Members bring a variety of experience but clearly thrive on new challenges and the eventual beauty in the outcomes of our joint enterprise. Neither Nik nor I have taught such elderly people before, but it has become a highlight of both our weeks. Members have said they really miss it and feel worse when we don't have a session. The commitment they have to learning new skills at their time of life is a humbling education for me.

After choir and a quick bite of lunch I then travel over moorland peaks to pick my three-year-old grandson up from pre-school. It is a harshly beautiful landscape which never looks the same. The weather is always bringing out a different colour or contour. The journey provides a moment of calm in a hectic week.

My grandson refreshes me and offers a delightful counterpoint to the online students and older choir members I learn from and with during the rest of the week. If he has the energy we go to the park or a friend's house to play. More often than not, we will go home to play with his toys. I basically follow his rhythms and follow his lead in terms of the activities we engage in and games we play. I feel that my work with professional educators is enhanced through my close contact with an outstanding school that models creative, holistic practice to which I am invited as a carer. This gives me another useful perspective on what schools can do for their communities. Thinking about this early years approach and its obvious delightful impact on my grandson and his peers informs my work across my week.

J. Voytilla

My typical day of work can be succinctly described as 'atypical'. Each day at an internationally travelling school can be a unique adventure, and when you add all the different hats that I wear into the mix, it can really become a bit of a crazy maze to get through. Let's take a look at last Tuesday for example which perhaps reveals a glimpse of what is 'typical' in my day.

The school day starts off at 8.30am in the city of Rabat, Morocco, our location for the next six weeks. On Tuesdays, I have first period free so I decide that it would be a great time to get some of my administrative duties out of the way, all of which involve accessing certain databases and online software. However, when I get to campus, the Wi-Fi is sluggish to the point of dinosaurs appearing in the browser window – not a very workable situation for a paperless school. I spend the next 30 minutes trying to figure out what is wrong with our system. I even tried resetting it several times, but to no avail. Finally, our awesome tech guru arrives and we determine that one of our students or staff must be being a vampire and downloading something huge, which is killing it for everyone else. After cycling around to all the classrooms and pleading to blank faces to please stop streaming and downloading, I am forced to give up on getting online because I now have ten minutes left to finalise my prep for the science class that I am covering for a colleague whose visa for Morocco has not been processed yet.

I run across the street to a local shop that was inexplicably closed the day before and in broken French manage to ask for some protractors (they measure angles) and after paying I then run back to campus and dig out the rest of my physics supplies; eight balls and a tape measure that I found super cheap in the medina souk during a humanities field trip last week. They are all mixed up in the laundry basket that contains all of the art supplies. One of the concerns with being in a travelling school is *stuff*, or rather the accumulation of it. When you are only in a country for 6–8 weeks of classes, it is wasteful to accumulate things, even organisational things that are normally found in every classroom in every school. We do our best to donate our supplies to good homes upon departure, but we have also learned to just make do in an attempt to avoid unnecessary and unsustainable waste. It's bad enough that we fly so much.

Teaching a physics unit to my colleague's Grade 10 class was my idea, and so I knew going in that it was going to polarise the class. Most students either love or hate physics, which they often confuse with maths. My plan with this bunch is strategic though. I already know that next semester when we go to Vancouver, Canada, that all subject classes are dissolving and instead we are piloting our all new Problem Based Learning (PBL) programme that we have never done before and that these kids are going to be in a MakerSpace four days a week. So, if I do not teach them any physics principles before then, there will either be more work ahead of me in Vancouver, or students will just miss out on half the spectrum of creative opportunity there. My only hope is that by using a creative and highly entertaining and differentiated concept modelling approach, I can engage at least 90 per cent of them in the three weeks I have to get through some basic kinematics, before my colleague arrives and shifts gears.

However, class suddenly ends 15 minutes early because the kind and generous women that run the language school have arrived and want to share a typical Moroccan breakfast with the entire school and take photos with everyone. Okay, I guess we will pick it up next class then. During this social event of snacking, tea drinking and horrible attempts at French, the dean of students finds me and I am reminded that I need to review the academic probation letter that was drafted earlier and that there is a new holistic development lesson that I need to study and deliver the next day. Next the IB coordinator finds me and informs me that lessons are cancelled the next day as there is a guest speaker and my afternoon meeting today is now two hours instead of one. I make notes on my mobile phone and hope I remember to read it later.

After our impromptu social event, my next class, enviro-science, starts 15 minutes late. As it is an IB class, we have to make the most of our six weeks here and grind our way through the curriculum. I spend 20 minutes with them briefing them on their lab assignment for the next day.

This is necessary because I will be covering my colleague's biology lab at the *same time* and I cannot lecture both classes simultaneously on the instructions. Once I have briefed them I give them a task and then slide over to the biology classroom, which is also happening at the same time today, and which I am also covering. I make sure that they are all using the online platform to get through their assignment, and then I brief them for 15 minutes on *their* lab for the next day. I then find them some resources for DNA replication and bounce back to my enviro class. This continues for another 50 minutes.

Thankfully, lunch seems to come early (due to our late start), and we all rush off to the restaurant that we have hired for our meals. I have to eat quickly because I have a meeting with the three teachers with whom I am co-teaching humanities. We also have an interdisciplinary magazine project on Morocco that has been going on for two weeks now and we still have to sort out the summative assessments.

After that, I race to the local café, and grab a *café au lait* to go and head up to my G12 enviro-science class who are mostly sick and remain zombies from finishing their extended essays over the weekend without sleeping. After a zesty 70 minutes of theatrics aimed at keeping them alive and engaged, my 'creativity, activity, service' (CAS) and extended essay (EE) workshop begins with Grade 11s. This is our space for planning service projects with the local communities, physical fitness plans, and creative field trips in general. It is also the only time that I have to prepare these students for their EEs and we spend at least half the class getting every-one to commit to a subject area and research question.

Finally my classes are done for the day and my now two-hour after-noon meeting commences. The meeting's sole purpose today is to find a way for ten staff to agree on how to structure a 7-week PBL interdisci-plinary project in Vancouver, using a MakerSpace that none of us have ever seen, involving some staff and students that have little or no PBL experience. I excuse myself near the beginning of the session and go and get myself another coffee.

Reflections

To put together these reflection sections we read the separate narratives to each other jotting down notes as we listened. We then tried to pull common themes or contradictions. The first thing that struck us about our 'typical' days in education was that there was no day that was typical.

Several of the authors state this explicitly and simply describe a single day as a symbol of a typical day.

We also realised that we educate in a wide range of places and spaces – from the souks of Morocco to community meeting rooms in Yorkshire, from purpose-built schools escaping the smog of Bangalore to hotel conference rooms around the world. But wherever we are teaching there is a common structure or flow to the day. Daily rhythms punctuated by food, often a piece of fruit on the hoof, or a swiftly grabbed cup of coffee. Some of us follow timetables laid down by the curriculum or the school organisation while some of us have timetabled ourselves as a way of structuring our day to make sure we stay on some kind of track. It was also clear to us that while all our educational spaces are set clearly in a local context they are influenced by the global context; either in terms of the global influence of education systems on each other, or simply through our life experiences as global educators.

We realised that all of us need to have committed teams around us – other adults who support us in our teaching, who plan and teach with us, or who support the learners we are working with. We seem to thrive on such collaborative activity but also must draw on our own resources for much of the day and work on our own. Indeed, many of the narratives describe grabbing any break from teaching as a chance to continue planning or complete marking, or collect resources. We wondered when a teacher's day ends. It certainly isn't when the students leave the space. Maybe more coffee is grabbed but planning for the next day, or the next project, starts in earnest as teaching finishes.

We commented that life in schools in the UK seemed to be more bound by administration and surveillance than it is in international schools. There was much less emphasis on extra-curricular activity for example and more of a sense of a teacher being embattled. We quickly realised that the international schools from which most of the stories emanate are fee-paying schools which might feel directly responsible to parents rather than feel they are being monitored by the state. The question that remains is: do schools which are monitored closely by a state feel less responsible to their learners and parents?

All of our educational lives would not be possible without all-pervasive technology. We have tutorials with students via Skype or virtual learning portals, students download their lessons and upload their work, presentations are constructed and shared using presentation software; and when the technology breaks down we are left struggling to carry on or having to find innovative ways to solve the problem.

Finally, there is a sense of personal growth in these narratives, of educators learning alongside their students and of pride when we see the results of our endeavour.

Figure 4.1 Graphical summary: My day in education.

Commonplace book: Entry 4

Try to describe a typical day in your teaching life.

How is it similar and how is it different from the authors' 'typical days'?

Chapter 5

Our best teachers

Let's make a calculation. We probably spend six years in primary education. For many of us that means at least six different teachers although in some countries there is more continuity than this. Then we move into secondary education. At this stage we probably have a different teacher for each subject that we study and this teacher may well change every year. You may then have had a driving instructor, a sports coach, a dance teacher or someone to teach you a musical instrument. It wouldn't be a surprise if there were over 50 people who, at some stage in your life, you could call your teacher.

It was a surprise that when we started to discuss our memories of our best teachers some of us couldn't remember anyone who we would describe as 'best'. To those of the group who did have favourite teachers this seemed extraordinarily sad. They could think of many individual teachers who had developed skills and understandings that we use every day to make sense of the world and to engage with the world. All of us, however, could remember someone who had made a real difference to our lives by making a genuine connection with us. It was this connection that enabled genuine learning to take place.

Lucy Cooker

Between 1981 and 1986, from the ages of 11 to 16, I attended a small comprehensive school on the very east coast of the UK in a seaside town called Sheringham. One of the teachers at the school was everybody's favourite teacher. Mr Sanpher taught biology and sex education. He also used to direct and produce musical shows and every Christmas would write and direct the school pantomime. He was young, had floppy black hair and was always a bit scruffy (but, of course, dressing well doesn't mean you teach well). He brought creativity and inspiration to the celebratory school productions, but also to any everyday biology lesson.

I loved Mr Sanpher's classes because they were funny. He was witty and would use humour effectively to engage us and keep our attention through 50 minutes of osmosis or photosynthesis or parasitic organisms. If we weren't paying attention he would gently tease us and bring us back to the focus of the lesson. In most classes I enjoyed the interaction and the practical aspects of learning: speaking French; carrying out experiments in chemistry; looking at maps in geography; but in biology my favourite parts of the lesson were listening to Mr Sanpher talk to the whole class. He brought the subject alive and knew how to reach out to every student. He wanted all of us to succeed and he believed we could and would succeed.

Sex education is probably still not easy to teach. Certainly in the 1980s in the midst of the HIV/AIDS epidemic it was a challenging but vitally important subject. Mr Sanpher taught it with a great deal of pragmatism and candour. As a shy 15-year-old I always felt grateful that he didn't seek to embarrass us, and that his straightforward but humorous approach brought a sense of ease and laughter to the topic.

My own teaching style is not at all similar to Mr Sanpher's. I do not feel comfortable talking to a class for a long period of time (and such a style of teaching is not compatible with my personal theory of learning). Nor can I be as consistently and reliably funny as he was. Instead, I use a lot of small-group work and interactive elements. Where I hope I have modelled myself on Mr Sanpher is in having the belief that every student can succeed.

Mr Sanpher was everybody's favourite teacher because he loved what he did. Reflecting back now on our lessons, I realise it wasn't biology or pantomimes that he loved, but teaching children and teenagers and releasing the potential in all of us.

Tony Cotton

I had taken piano lessons on and off for 30 years by the time I turned up at my new teacher's house. I knocked on the door tentatively. It had been years since my last lesson. I was an adult and could see through the window that the pupil before me was a young girl. I felt like the new boy on his first day at school. During this first lesson my new teacher was dismissive of the value of examinations. I had suggested I might work towards my 'grades' as a measure of my progress. He suggested this was pointless and that I could measure my progress in terms of the complexity of pieces I 'mastered' and the enjoyment I got out of playing for pleasure. During the first lesson he altered my fingering on a piece of music I played to him. He explained that the fingering I was using was making the piece sound 'clumsy and forced'. I was playing the correct notes but as he said, 'playing music is about much more than playing the right notes'. When I came to play the piece using his new fingering I couldn't make my fingers obey my brain, the notes fell out in a jumble. I felt useless. I wanted to practise one hand at a time, as this was the system I had got used to. My teacher suggested an alternative. 'Always practice with both hands', he said (it felt like an order), 'find a speed at which you can play the piece accurately using two hands and gradually speed up as you get used to the piece'. I remember leaving this lesson confused but willing to give it a go. My teacher seemed to offer me a new way of learning and a new motivation to learn. After all, the way I had been trying to learn in the past hadn't been effective so why not try something new?

I remember two lessons which cemented my relationship with my teacher and gave me confidence in myself as a learner. The first is when I had changed the time for my lesson and arrived slightly early. The learner before me was another adult which surprised me but made me feel less unusual. I realised I wasn't the only adult having lessons. At the end of this lesson the teacher took over at the piano stool and played the piece that my peer had been struggling with. It was beautiful. My confidence in my teacher shot up, as did my motivation. I wanted to be able to play like that. I wanted my teacher to show me how. I remember calculating how many piano lessons I could have in the next ten years and setting myself the target of being able to play 'like that' in ten years' time.

During my lesson, my teacher commented that he liked teaching adults as they had a musicality that young children didn't have. A musicality born out of experience and listening. This made me feel confident in my current ability and allowed me to bring something new to the piano. During the lesson, he produced a new piece for me to take away and asked me to sight read the piece. He said that if I could sight read this piece I would 'move up' a book. I did (I'm sure my teacher knew I would be able to), and left the lesson with a new book in my bag and a skip in my step (literally – I still remember the feeling).

My second vivid memory is a lesson just before a Christmas break. I remember feeling relaxed and content as I arrived. I have always been a sucker for feeling uplifted by Christmas decorations. We were tying up a few loose ends and I was to perform a piece that I had been working on for several weeks for a 'tick'. This was a ritual which signalled when my teacher felt I had mastered a piece. I would play the piece through as if in performance and if I was happy with my performance, yes, self-assessment, I would be rewarded with a tick in the book next to the title of the piece. You will have noticed that even adult learners like ticks in their books. He then asked, 'Have we ever played a duet? As it's Christmas we could try a carol'. We went over to the grand piano. I was nervous and excited. What an honour to play on such a beautiful instrument. He put a piece of music up. 'It starts in E', he said. And off he went. I have no memory of what the piece was but a clear memory of the feeling of exhilaration I felt as I kept up, clinging on by the tips of my fingers, feeling as though I was really playing the piano. I realised I was sight reading, feeling for the notes without looking down, listening for pitch and tone, all the things that I had been working at for so long, and I was doing them without having time to think. It was the most exciting five minutes in my piano playing career.

Edward Emmett

The PGCEi run by the University of Nottingham is my example of best-ever teaching. The law in Thailand had changed and a friend and I had been talking about needing to take the qualification to remain teaching here. I was nervous about the requirements as I did not think I had the necessary entry qualifications; I have written earlier about my lack of engagement with my degree. But I was accepted on the course because of my experience which I was delighted about but also daunted by. I felt sure that the tutors would find out I could not do it.

The moment when I felt like I could really do it was when Helen (one of the tutors) invited me to attend a meeting with other dyslexic students in a private room; it reminded me of my Year 6 teacher pulling me aside to tell me I could do it when everything was falling apart after my Mum's sudden death. I have never had confidence in my own abilities, always hated school when teachers didn't take any notice of me. I need someone to believe in me; everyone does.

Handing in the first draft for the first essay to be marked was really frightening. I was expecting all the feedback to be negative, but instead I was supported to build on my ideas using comment boxes next to what I had written and this really helped me keep going and redraft. Everything

I had asked for that would help me structure my writing was being used. I just don't think I'd had very good teachers before and I had never had relevant feedback that was meaningful to me, but here I was in control and was given what I asked for.

I felt confident with all the tutors on the PGCEi course in Bangkok and this was honestly the first time I had ever felt confidence in education. I also loved online discussion and Skype meetings to support my thinking. When Helen, Tony and Lucy, the course tutors contacted me to write this book I was delighted, but had to overcome some doubts planted by friends who said things like, 'Why would you want to do that, it's just extra work?' I didn't see it like that it's an opportunity to carry on working with these tutors.

Lisa Fernandes

All through school for many of my classmates and me, the learning of our second language in school was the bane of our existence. For most of us, the second language choice was between Hindi (the national language of India) or Kanada (our state language). Even though I was a fairly diligent student and enjoyed working hard at my studies, I felt very vulnerable when it came to Hindi. Unlike many of the north Indian students, I did not speak Hindi at home, and had to spend many hours working on the grammar, vocabulary and pronunciation, at the expense of my other lessons and free time. The classes were very structured, strictly based on the textbook which was full of archaic, flowery poems and stories that had no meaning for me. The teacher, to be fair to her, had a large portion of the curriculum to complete and we were made to write out her questions followed by her answers, which we then learnt by heart for the test. I had to learn long lists of verbs and vocabulary by rote, and had to attend a Hindi 'tuition' class thrice a week in the evenings after school, just to ensure I passed the subject. The tuition teacher, besieged by too many students per batch, was rough and stern and did not think twice about throwing me and my Hindi book out of the class, when I hadn't prepared enough by her standards. On more than one occasion I had to retrieve my book from the vicinity of her fierce Alsatian. Needless to say, I found learning Hindi a huge waste of time throughout school. I consequently hated the class, the language and by default the teacher.

Naturally, when I finally got a choice to switch to French for my pre-university years, I grabbed it. During the summer holidays that followed, my Mum signed up for me to attend the local Alliance Française de Bangalore.

The teacher who took the intensive summer session was a young, animated Frenchman. I was not enamoured by the fact that I would have to attend summer school. However, from the start the teacher's easy, welcoming manner set the tone for the class and I found myself looking forward to the one and a half hour sessions twice a week. Through the weeks and months that followed we were introduced to France, her culture, her cuisine, to wine and cheese parts of the country, from vineyards to Versailles, as we learnt our verbs and vocabulary and carried on conversations with our peers. We had cook-outs, drama sessions, went to the theatre, museums and outdoor markets. Our course textbook listed the bits of grammar that we had to work on, but the lessons were built on authentic scenarios which, as a teenager, I was able to relate to and significantly contribute to in the small groups that we invariably worked in. The teacher, through conversations with me, encouraged me to continue learning French and I grew to love the language and culture. This positive experience with learning another language helped open my mind to new methods and attitudes towards learning. My French teacher showed me how important it was to plan engaging and challenging lessons that were authentic and significant in the lives of learners.

It was clear through the course that each student's individual interest would guide their learning. So, many years later when I returned to India with my own children I was relieved that my daughter did not have to go through the process of learning a language by rote. She had a choice and took French and she enjoys as much as I did the rich learning of a new language. I was encouraged to be a risk taker, an inquirer and a lifelong learner through the course and that is something I want to encourage in every lesson I teach.

Han Wei

I want to talk about two teachers. There are so many good teachers in my life but these two have inspired me differently. The first one was my mathematics teacher at primary school. She was a new teacher but I really liked her because she inspired my pure love of mathematics. She taught me for four years. I'd had another teacher previously for two years. I loved mathematics for so many years because of her. The way she taught was very different from the traditional teacher. She used a lot of different tools and technology to help us. For example, in my home town at that time there wasn't a lot of technology but she used a projector.

It was the first time anyone had used a projector with us in school and she used it very smartly, to show us how to draw a graph. She also made lots of resources to show us how to make a calculation. She made a paper clock and taught us how to calculate the time by showing us how the paper needles moved. She showed us the different ways we could get answers and this really motivated me and made me realise mathematics was interesting and beautiful. Moreover, the way she communicated was different. She was quite strict but she respected us too. In other classes we had to raise hands to answer questions. In this class we could answer questions at any time we wanted so I felt free in her class and I felt comfortable. She was like a friend. Whenever we had problems we could talk to her. Over my whole life so far, only she has inspired me and helped me to find a pure interest in one subject.

The second teacher was my lecturer and tutor at the University of Nottingham in the UK. He showed me a very different way of teaching. I guess this is because he was from the West and was educated in western culture. He was one of the best teachers because I really enjoyed each lesson. He always asked us questions and every time we wanted to answer we were free to do so, or to ask him questions. The class was more like a discussion rather than just delivering knowledge. It really helped me to develop my critical thinking. It was a Masters course and I had never had this experience before. When I was in China at university, teaching was more like chalk and talk – the teacher would stand in front and teach us knowledge and show us materials – it was like that all through my education. My tutor in Nottingham focused more on discussion. He wanted to know our opinions and wanted to encourage us when we had good ideas. He pushed us to take challenges and didn't really comment a lot when we had discussions. However, the way he commented was tricky because he didn't say whether we were right or wrong, but just prompted us with questions or ideas. We didn't find out if our answers were right or not. Only later, when I did research on my ideas, did I find out whether my thinking was appropriate. I really appreciated the style of his teaching and it made me become more open and to think about things differently.

Cassius Lubisi

My best teacher, without a shadow of a doubt, was the late Sister Dorothea Derse who was also principal of my high school. She studied for her degrees at the University of Notre Dame in the US and had two Masters degrees, in mathematics and physics. She was a highly intelligent teacher, very strict but very fair and gave us the opportunity to learn and construct our own knowledge in physics, chemistry and mathematics.

I recall once she gave us a theorem and I looked at it and I thought it was too specific. I thought I could generalise it even further. I showed it to her and proved to her that it was an underestimation of the power of the theorem. She was delighted. She was a very empathetic teacher. In some ways she treated us like we were her children.

She was the reason I followed mathematics. I had hoped that I would return to Inkanama and teach with her there but at the time the school was suffering financial problems because there were dwindling donations from Germany.

The way I teach mathematics and my attitude towards mathematics can be traced back to her. She believed that all children could learn mathematics. In primary school I was told it was only the elite that could understand it but she taught me differently. She proved this by teaching those who were the least gifted in mathematics and achieving incredible results. She taught them to excel. She taught me to democratise mathematics education so that it is fairly distributed across all sections of the population and not distributed only to an elite determined largely by race and class.

Haana Sandy

I realised as I was writing the final drafts of my previous passage in this book that I had been really negative about teachers and school experiences, so it was nice to be asked to write about my 'best teacher' as I found, to my surprise, there were several to choose from. I had a horrible Grade 1 teacher and did not get off to a good start at school, but then my Grade 2/3 teacher had a positive impact, she was not formal or always telling me off. I felt comfortable and safe with her. Similarly my middle school mathematics, science and Farsi teachers were all lovely, hard-working and caring. I enjoyed their teaching and felt safe to make mistakes. One clear memory of them is the chalk dust all over their clothes as they were most definitely 'chalk and talk' teachers.

The teacher who made the most impact on me was Mr Taamay (pronounced Tarmey). He was tall with grey hair and he showed his warm personality through his teaching style. He was an excellent teacher with a naturally 'fun' personality and a talent for turning a hard subject into a great story. He made even hard things seem easy to understand. I love algebra and always remember his explanations – he used language to engage young learners – 'See, this one vanishes like an alien'. Mathematics is a serious subject but he was very charismatic, we listened to him intently; we listened to him more than any other teacher.

His daughters were the same age as me and I found out later as I got to know them that he was a caring father and husband, he was lovable.

Can you learn to be a charismatic teacher, to be more fun in lessons? Perhaps it comes from the way your life turns out, but sometimes I wish I was more fun, like Mr Taamay. I am not as articulate in English as I am in Farsi and so I think I come across as too serious in my classroom in Leeds, but I try to explain in language that children can connect with. I have a joke and try to make children feel safe to learn. Some children have warmed to my style and will ask for me if they have a problem.

Helen Toft

I have come to notice that the kind of lecturer I am may well be modelled on a young academic who taught me a module in twentieth-century literature 40 years ago. Reading literature at university was a privilege I accessed after gaining better than expected A level results. On the day I received my results a deputy head at my school took me to one side and said I would be wasted on the course I had accepted. He said that I needed to try for university and after a few phone calls I had accepted a place at Sheffield University to study English literature.

In the final year of the course I could choose from a number of modules. I chose a module studying Raymond Chandler, the American detective writer made famous in Bogart and Bacall films, taught by Brian (I forget his surname), fresh out of university himself. He was hugely nervous on a personal level but when he was in the Chandler zone he was transformed, challenging, supporting, laughing and hugely excited about the writing he was so intimate with. He seemed to be a mixture of excited that talking about his main love was 'work' and nervous that he might be found out. Perhaps he was concerned that Chandler might not be seen as a proper topic for study at this level; he was blazing a trail in true innovator style. Above all I loved his ability to step back and let us argue and develop a point together. He seemed enthralled by our discoveries.

At a one-to-one, tutorial level, discussion was awkward. I was uncertain about my own ideas and he was painfully shy so we stumbled through only one of these meetings, with me being relieved that at least the power dynamic between us was on more of an equal footing than with other more experienced, but I found rather pompous, tutors. And I thrived in seminar groups where we worked collaboratively with people who saw many other meanings in the words on the page, encouraging us to articulate and develop them as a group, with Brian learning from us himself.

All these years on I am not sure he knew much about the theory of teaching, but I wonder if he had a great role model himself as well as him being extraordinarily well read and open to new learning. I now also know that Brain was gay and although I hadn't realised this it might have been why I felt 'safe' with him in contrast to other lecturers who had made unwelcome advances. Until that point I had felt I was not able to learn well from a teacher who didn't 'warm' to me and know me well, but maybe I had 'come of age' as a learner.

This experience has influenced the way I run seminar or full cohort sessions at university in that it has given me permission to stimulate ideas and discussion but not lead the thinking – to let understandings be created by group interaction. I have also learnt that you don't have to be absolutely perfect at every aspect of your role to maintain the interest and dedication of mature students – they have so many capabilities themselves and understand the multiple pressures of teaching so well. Finally, it taught me that personal integrity and security in one's identity are just as valuable as interpersonal skills.

J. Voytilla

When I think back to my educational history, I must admit that it is a bit fuzzy now. However, there is one experience with a particular teacher that still resonates to this day. During high school, I was certainly not what you would call a good student. In fact, I was often 'absent', to be found carousing about the city with my mates who were also cutting class. Carol Ogilvie was one of my high school English teachers, and probably the one person on the staff that I took seriously and respected. What made her stand out for me was not merely her delivery style or easy-going manner, or even her youth. It was her 'realness', which is hard to describe and break down without using the other teachers in the school as a foil. Unlike most, Carol was not burned out and jaded when she led the class, not blankly staring at rows of numbers as she repeated the same tired old speeches from yesteryear. When she looked at you, she did so in the eye, and she actually *saw* you.

For various reasons during this period of my life, I found myself quite disengaged from school, and a lot more engaged with the more chaotic elements around town. This is not to say I was a part of a socio-economically disenfranchised group of young thugs, but rather I was caught somewhere in between that extreme and the more traditional social banality of high school life, a sort of duality of outsider looking in *and* an insider looking out. Carol seemed to take an interest in me, and to this day I am not sure why. I can recall having numerous conversations with her outside of class, and over time they started to drift into more personal territory. With the gift of hindsight now – especially as an educator myself – I can see that she was probably seeing something of my home life on my face during the day, and was beginning to gently probe, in her own way, as to what might have been going on with me.

I have to admit, it freaked me out a little bit. I mean, isn't it *us* against *them*? What the hell was this *caring* all about? Around this time I started backing even further away from school for a time, disappearing with my mates off campus and not even bothering to turn in major assignments that did not immediately command my interest anymore. I was just floating by.

However, Carol was having none of that. I remember her tracking me down in the halls one day – I cannot remember how long it had been since I showed up to her English class – and demanding to know when she was going to see my essay on some-such book whose name is now lost in the dusty annals of memory ... which absolutely stunned me! That essay was due two weeks ago! I likely mumbled something apologetic and barely coherent in reply, and then she carried on telling me how I had better get it in by the end of the week, and then with that she marched off, leaving me standing there stunned in my ripped jeans, unkempt long hair, and Led Zeppelin T-shirt. Before rounding a corner, she turned back once and looked at me again. 'Why?' was all my befuddled brain could think to ask. 'Because I am not giving up on you', was her reply and then she was gone.

I wrote that damn essay, and Carol Ogilvie chased me down for a few more too. I finally got myself sorted out the following year and started showing up for classes, even after moving out on my own, and even got myself into university. Several twists and turns later plus eight years and I even found myself beginning a teaching career.

I do not know what became of Ms Ogilvie, and I deeply regret turning away from her and not getting the chance to know her, but I am eternally grateful that she didn't turn away from me.

Reflections

The key themes leaped out of these narratives for us. Authenticity runs through all our experiences. Teachers who have a genuine love for the subject they are teaching and are experts in their field allows them to keep our interest, even when they are explaining complex ideas; and who are authentic in terms of their relationship with their students. We particularly remembered this, as we felt that genuine and sincere belief in us as a learner and as a human being. As J. says, 'When she looked at you, she did so in the eye, and she actually *saw* you'. Our best teachers all looked us in the eye, saw our potential, and knew what they could do to support us in developing our potential. They believed in us, they showed that they would never give up on us and as a result they enabled us to believe in ourselves.

There is also a sense of the role of the learner in developing our personal best teachers. Several of the stories suggest the taking of risks by the learner to move forward, whether this is Tony letting himself go at the piano keyboard or J. swallowing his pride and writing an essay; Ed taking a deep breath and enrolling on the PGCEi in Bangkok or Lisa taking on another foreign language in French.

We also realised that some of us remembered charismatic teachers, and carry a clear memory of what they looked like – Mr Sanpher with his floppy black hair; Mr Taamey, tall with grey hair or the animated young Frenchman who became Lisa's French teacher. These teachers remain vivid in the memory. For others, it wasn't the charisma of an individual that captured us but an intensity of emotion in feeling successful, in really learning something. Haana wonders if you can learn to be more charismatic and reflects on the way that she is developing her personal style to reflect some of the traits she recognises in her best teacher. Lucy realises that she doesn't need to teach like her best teacher to become the best teacher for some of her students.

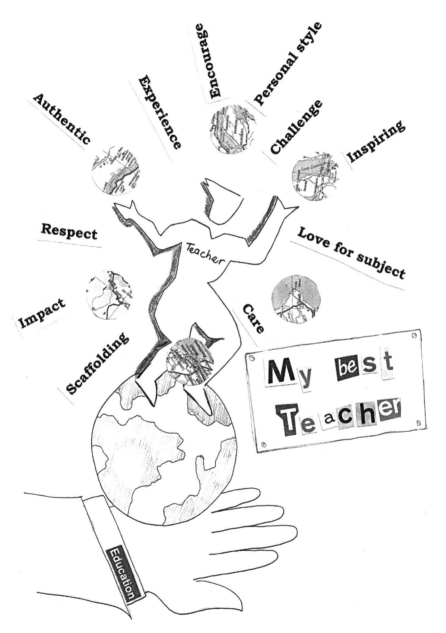

Figure 5.1 Graphical summary: Our best teachers.

Commonplace book: Entry 5

Who was your best teacher?

Write you own narrative below describing a time when you remember really succeeding as a learner

Chapter 6

Lessons learned

For the most part the narratives in this book draw on positive experiences of education. We explore what inspired and supported us. We celebrate those individuals in our lives who we can see in our current selves as teachers. This chapter is different. It is an acknowledgement that for some people schooling was a period of their lives characterised by fear and humiliation. Such negative feelings can remain with us for the rest of our lives and can leave individuals feeling distanced from formal schooling and suspicious of education.

We found this part of the book difficult to write. We were revisiting uncomfortable periods in our educational journeys. But we felt that it was important to take the time to work with these negative experiences as we believe that reflection on these, often quite painful, episodes can teach us important lessons about learning that we can draw on to inform our teaching.

Lucy Cooker

Earlier in the book, I mentioned briefly one of the more negative experiences I have had as a learner. At primary school, my teacher, Miss Mills, used to give us mental arithmetic tests. We all had to stand up, and were only allowed to sit down when we could answer a calculation correctly. It felt like an inevitability that I would be the last one left standing each time. The sense of exclusion and shame that I felt during this process has had an enduring effect on me and I would never knowingly pick on students in the same manner. I am always at pains to ensure students feel their learning environment is a safe and secure one, not somewhere where they will feel vulnerable and exposed.

Perhaps, as a consequence of my experiences in Miss Mills's class, I was never very confident in mathematics at school. I wanted to like mathematics and to see the beauty of mathematical formulae, but it felt like my brain could not see what it was meant to see. I tried hard, gained a Grade B at O level through learning strategies for passing the exams but I was never in control of the mathematics on the page in front of me. Having achieved a B I could then forget about mathematics at A level; but during my degree studies the terror of numbers came back to haunt me in mandatory statistics classes. Because of my lack of ability and confidence I was asked to join a remedial statistics class. Once again that sense of exclusion and shame returned. Now, through my teachers' eyes, I can see that although this was tertiary level education, the remedial class was a form of streaming or setting. I am a big advocate of mixed ability classes and I have always felt policies involving streaming, setting and banding are unhelpful at best, and at worst very damaging, in terms of the impact of such a policy on learners' self-belief and self-esteem.

One of the most salient lessons learned for me came as a new teacher rather than as a learner. I was working as a university teacher in Japan teaching English to undergraduates. These were students who had busy lives, they often had a long commute to university (sometimes up to three hours) and frequently worked late at night in a part-time job to help them pay tuition fees and earn living expenses. On this day, I was team teaching a sophomore class and working alongside a recently recruited colleague. The class had started, and we had got the lesson off to an upbeat start, when a student arrived 15 minutes late. This was not unusual. Students often had apologies relating to their part-time jobs or long commutes. I drew attention to the student by greeting him publicly and making a rather sarcastic comment about his tardiness.

My colleague was appalled, and pointed out that I had no understanding of the student's circumstances, or what had caused him to be late. He told me that had this happened in the UK, where he had recently been working, teachers would not comment but would simply welcome the student and address the reasons for the lateness in a more discreet manner after the class had ended. On hearing this feedback, I was embarrassed and mortified by how I had behaved. I thought I was doing what teachers do. I expect I was unwittingly mimicking some of the teachers I had had in my earlier schooling. It took my colleague's observation to help me realise that not only had I potentially shamed the student but I had contravened my own personal values, that wearing a 'teacher's hat' did not mean I had to stop being me. This experience has remained with me ever since, and has helped me learn that part of being a good teacher is being an authentic human being.

Tony Cotton

I am a passionate advocate for all-attainment grouping in schools. I believe that we learn most effectively in diverse groups. Diverse groups mean a diversity of experience, of prior learning, of ways of looking at things. Surely such a group is much better equipped to problem-solve or research than a group put together through some false sense of homogeneity. This view has informed my teaching from early in my career. I took a job in a school purely because they taught all the students in all-attainment groups, even in mathematics which is my subject. Whenever I work alongside teachers in schools now I insist that we organise the students in all-attainment groups whatever the usual classroom arrangement might be.

As well as knowing that this approach is supported by a large body of research evidence I think that two episodes in my own primary school career taught me very early on about the myth of using 'ability' to support approaches to differentiation and progression.

The first: I am five. I can read, I can't remember how I learned but I can remember that I was a fluent reader by the time I started infant school. I was somewhat confused when I first arrived at school as I wasn't allowed to read any book that I chose. I accepted this at first, after all this was school, not home. I realised that there was a reading scheme that we were expected to follow in order. The scheme was called 'The Pirates' and each book was about a different pirate – the red pirate, the blue pirate and so on. I have a clear memory of the day when I went to the front of the class to find the purple pirate as that was the next book I had to read. Unfortunately, there were no copies left. I suggested to the teacher, Miss Moss, that I should read the black pirate and then come back to the purple pirate. Angrily she told me to go back to my desk and reread the book I had just finished. She seemed to suggest I wasn't ready for the complexity of the black pirate until I had learned the lessons of the purple pirate. 'But I can read!' I pleaded, 'it doesn't make any difference what order I read them in'. Outbursts such as this tended to be interpreted as arrogance rather than educational debate so I ended up back at my desk flicking through the unmitigated dullness of a book I had already read.

Later that same week. The register is being taken just before quiet reading time. Miss Moss reaches my name. 'Cotton', she says. They were very formal at Greetby Hill Primary School in 1964. 'Present, Miss Moose', I reply, straight faced. Miss Moss visibly pales. 'I beg your pardon?, 'Yes, Miss Moose', I reply again. The rest of the class start to giggle. Miss Moss looks up from the register and orders me to leave the classroom until I can 'learn some manners'. I leave the classroom and make my way to the library where I choose from the array of glorious reading available to a literate five-year-old.

The second: I am now 11. I am still at Greetby Hill Primary School but by now we have moved up to the third floor. There are 42 11-year-olds in the classroom and we share double desks. We are allocated our seats every week by the results of mental arithmetic tests. The 'brightest' pupils are allocated the desk nearest to the teacher, the 'dull-witted' while away their time in the far corner of the classroom. I have always enjoyed and been successful in mathematics and by this stage have realised that I can always get full marks in the weekly tests. I have also calculated that if I get six questions wrong I get to sit in the first row of the classroom but at the end of the row, away from the teacher, and next to the door. This was my favourite seat. I seemed invisible to the teacher as long as I kept quiet, and more importantly I could get out of the door first at playtime and be first in the queue for sticky buns (yes – we are in the days before healthy eating was invented). In fact, I made a little extra pocket money by buying buns for those in the class who ended up at the back of the queue and charging them 'a penny for going'.

Edward Emmett

My secondary schooling was totally chaotic. All sorts of terrible things happened and I had to develop an ability not to be a violent or abusive student, but not be too good either or I would have been bullied so I decided to be 'in the middle' of the trouble we all caused.

The school was awful and went into 'special measures'. This is the worst judgement that a school can receive from government inspectors. Many of the staff left as a result of this judgement and we had many different teachers in each subject with lots of cover teachers. They had also started to rebuild the school so our lessons were all in temporary classrooms. Things got so bad that a student once set a table on fire in science. That was when I thought to myself, 'this is just mad'.

The incidents I want to focus on occurred in every Spanish lesson. We would be very unruly. Our main aim was to make the teacher cry. Once we achieved our objective we would jump out of the first floor window and run off. No one ever did anything about it. We would 'bunk off' school and miss all our lessons later that day and would never get into trouble about it. I think the problem was that none of our form tutors (homeroom teachers) taught us for a subject. They didn't care how we were behaving with anyone else. I did have an art teacher for my form tutor who really cared and would have followed it up, but he left I think. He was so nice. From then on, all we had to do was turn up for morning registration; if you weren't there for that you had to stay for detention on a Friday for the number of minutes you were late, but not for anything you did wrong in a lesson. There were never any full classes, loads of kids didn't turn up to lessons with excuses like 'Oh, I've got to go and play the drums' and no one ever checked if you actually did have drum lessons.

Being bullied would have been worse than not learning anything. It has made me streetwise and I can understand children when they behave a bit like I used to. I coach a football team of boys who are nowhere near as bad as I was, but I understand them, can relate to them when other teachers are shocked at their behaviour. I did the same thing. I tell the boys that their behaviour 'doesn't make them cool' and don't let it get to me. I don't think I would be able to handle how I and my peers behaved, but if I had to I would give it a go, depending on the circumstances.

Lisa Fernandes

Rather than focus on a teacher who led to difficult learning experiences for me I want to talk about a more general experience of education which, at the time, I found very difficult. Earlier in the book, I mentioned that I studied in a convent school. I was a diligent student and worked hard at all aspects, including the extra-curricular activities that required staying back after school for play rehearsals and inter-school competitions. In tenth grade, I ran for the post of head girl of the school and missed winning by 19 votes. I was really upset and disappointed. At that time, our school received an invitation from the Altrusa club of Washington State (USA) to sponsor an exchange student. To make up for my disappointment in not becoming head girl, my teachers asked me if I would like to go for a year to the United States, as an exchange student.

I was delighted and managed to convince my parents to let me go, against my father's better judgement. For the first time in my life, I left India and travelled across the globe to Olympia, the capital city of Washington State, to live with two American families for six months at a stretch. I was to attend the local public school. There were very few Indian families in the area at that time, and the high school students initially did not know if I could speak English or communicate with them. Some of the students presumed I was Hindu and worshipped the cow and I would get a few 'moos' and jeers as I walked through the hallways. I remember, especially in the beginning, feeling lonely and sad. I realised that the students had had limited exposure to students from other countries and cultures and this manifested itself in their stereotyping of Indians in general. This led me to work extra hard to prove that I could read, write and spell better than the other students in my class. My host parents and my teachers, Mr Gerst (an American history teacher) and the biology teacher in particular, were people I could relate to and I ended up having a wonderful year as an exchange student and making some really close friends.

Now many years later as a homeroom teacher in a truly international environment in India, I sometimes hear primary students imitating the host culture (Indian) accent and the signature head shaking. Initially I used to get annoyed and put them in their place, sharply. However, now I realise they don't really mean to racially condemn Indians but just feel the need to explore new sounds, sights and smells. With students from 30 different countries and teachers from 15 different countries, there are plenty of languages and accents, with 75 per cent of the students learning English as an additional language. So now, I welcome any interest in the host culture and open the discussion to allow the students to inquire deeper into our diverse Indian culture so rich in language and tradition.

Han Wei

When I just started to learn chemistry in junior high school (JHS), I was really interested in it and I was good at it. But later on my feeling about chemistry changed because of my teacher's reaction to my misbehaviour – I was told off by my teacher in front of everyone and that was embarrassing. I had always been a good student since primary school and I behaved well in the class. Even though sometimes I was a bit naughty, teachers generally just reminded me or talked to me privately. However, this time I was told off in front of the whole class which was beyond my expectation. I felt everyone was looking at me and laughing at me. I felt the teacher did not need to do it that way. I did not like the teacher any more but I was still good at chemistry. But after a few months, the same thing happened again. That was when I started to dislike the teacher and didn't enjoy any circumstances when he was involved, including chemistry lessons. I gave up the subject in the end after getting low scores.

I also had a similar experience with my students because the way I spoke to them was quite negative. I had a student who was British-born Chinese, and his cousins came to live with him for the whole summer holiday. After the summer holiday his personality had changed and he'd become more difficult and negative. Whatever we talked about he found the negative angle. I tried to tell him off and say he shouldn't talk too loudly, and he should sit quietly, but this didn't get a good result. After I told him off he became very aggressive and negative about learning the lesson. Previously he'd been the best student in the class, and had been a very fast learner. After the summer holiday his behaviour issues came to the fore. I tried to talk to him privately, but to no avail. I spoke to his mother, but his mother had a lot of problems at home and asked me for help, saying he didn't listen to her either. He had a sister in the class, and she was very good at learning, but both had become negative and difficult to manage. His sister was very shy, but she enjoyed learning and I encouraged her a lot, but during this semester she also became very difficult to manage. She lost her shyness and became much more outgoing, but that meant she talked too much during the class.

I tried to tell both of them off, but they became increasingly aggressive. Later, I set a rule for the whole class. We talked about the rules and set them together, what we should do in the classroom and what we shouldn't do. If a student had misbehaved there would be consequences. For example, they would have to go and talk to the head teacher or change classes. We made a deal. After that, the whole class was much more manageable, but those two still had issues and were very different from before.

These things made me think about my own experiences and how being told off in front of the class made me feel very uncomfortable, and how the opinion of the teacher influences the reaction of the students. As a result, I tried to motivate them by trying a different way of talking to them. When they answered my questions I encouraged them by saying 'good try' or something similar, even if the answer wasn't correct. I would also tell them which answer was correct or not. I would encourage them by saying 'well done' or, if they misbehaved, I would say, 'You've done so well today it would be good if you could keep that up'. The whole class changed and the reactions of the other students changed and the class generally became more positive. So motivation and talking to students in a positive way is very important.

Cassius Lubisi

One has had lots of negative experiences because one went through a system of education that was designed to keep black people in their place in apartheid. The architect of apartheid was a gentleman called Hendrick Verwoerd. He was once prime minister and was killed in parliament in 1966 by a Greek immigrant. He was the ideological architect of apartheid. One of the things he said in 1953 when he introduced Bantu education, designed for the black African population, was: 'What is the use of teaching a Bantu child mathematics because it has no use for it?' He also said, 'We must teach the Bantu to be hewers of wood and drawers of water'.

So, what we were being taught in school and the methodology that was used to teach us was different from the experience of white children. Our system was based on the notion of 'authority'. Children had to respect the authority of the teacher whose authority was drawn from a Calvinist god. We basically just had to memorise things which was not something I liked. We had to memorise crazy things like verses from the Bible. If we said them incorrectly this would be followed by a serious beating. The teachers just beat you up really. Memorising verses from the Bible was not my strong point so I used to hide behind other children. When we had to chorus the verses, I would just move my lips and not say anything.

Mathematics was also taught in a formulaic, memorisation style. You had to know your multiplication table like you know the palm of your hand. In this case children used to hide behind me as I could memorise my tables very well. Although I was good at this I didn't enjoy it. I hated memorisation and hated going to school.

We also studied agriculture. The subject could not be called agriculture really; it was basically gardening for white families. We would be set to work in the gardens of our white compatriots. We were taught gardening, how to plant seeds and how to look after them as they grew but even if we did these things correctly sometimes what we were planting did not grow correctly. We would get beaten for that too. We thought, 'we can't be god now and influence how plants grow. If it isn't growing it isn't our fault'. But we would still get a beating. It was harsh, extremely harsh. It was serious abuse. Fortunately, when I went to Inkamana School there was no corporal punishment and I was liberated from the burden of beatings.

Haana Sandy

The story of my journey is not all good, though I am in a much stronger place now. I had a really difficult time on the teacher training course in England, not on my teaching placements. I did my placements in two different schools and I was really confident. It was writing the essays that I struggled with and if I didn't have Tony's (Cotton) support in writing these essays I am not sure I would have passed the course.

I did pass, and got a job straightaway after my very first interview. I started teaching in a really challenging school. Teaching in a tough school is hard, full stop; but this experience pushed me into the darkest place of my career so far. This school was in a deprived, mainly white area of Leeds. I could feel an atmosphere of hostility towards me. Not only were the students racist and abusive, calling me 'suicide bomber' for example, but the staff didn't take any incidents I reported seriously or give me any support. I had an inexperienced mentor who was not supportive at all and reported every incident I alerted her to as if she was against me. The head of department began by believing her, but later he realised that she twisted stories and so he took over my mentoring. Unfortunately he left the school shortly after that and as a result I was given a mentor from a different department.

As a newly qualified teacher (NQT) I had to undergo regular observations. Often, I was given no notice and these observations came out of the blue. I think this is unacceptable and it is in fact not allowed for an NQT who is still under supervision and requires regular support. It was as if they knew I was not fully aware of the system and policies and that I did not know my rights as an NQT. Eventually I was overwhelmed by the lack of support. Working in a different country with no experience of how the system works had pushed me into a very difficult situation.

At that stage I thought, 'What am I going to do, am I really going to be able to be a teacher in England?' My union told me to leave the school so I resigned and ended up with no job for a few months. It was the most negative experience in my career but I was determined that these obstacles should not defeat me. This is one of many challenges in my life that I have faced and I knew that I should have the strength to fight against injustice and didn't want to give up. Even so this was a big battle inside me. It was even more difficult as I didn't know how and from where to get support and to seek justice. I tried my best, but deep down I felt suppressed; I was trying to flourish but I was being pushed down into the ground. However, looking back, I feel like those horrible experiences did make me more resilient.

After two or three months away from the classroom, I found the strength to get a job as a cover teacher in different schools. This began to broaden my experience. I had a chance to experience different schools and as a result my eyes were gradually opened. I was working at my current school as a long-term cover teacher and they asked me to fill a permanent post without an interview. This really boosted my confidence again. Unfortunately the employment regulations meant that I did have to go through an interview process for what is now my current job. I got it.

Helen Toft

By chance Tony has recently been inspired by a primary school that issues every child with a box of Cuisenaire® Rods to play with from the age of four. Every day free play with these beautifully designed, damage-resistant plastic teaching aids is encouraged by all staff, eventually leading to sophisticated calculations and 'proofs' using these inspirational tools.

He bought some sets with which to inspire early years staff to support their development in teaching mathematics. I realised as I touched them that they brought back strong memories. The intensity was striking. Although they are now made, not of smooth colourful wood, but a different material, they felt familiar and beautifully sculptured. Easy to manipulate for modelling a calculation, they represent my only positive memory of mathematics at school. Sadly they are also the symbol of my worst memory. Starting 'big' school was traumatic for me. I don't remember attending a nursery school in preparation, but my mum must have taken me to some sort of playgroup. I certainly played with neighbours' children during my early childhood. The formality and expectations of my first classroom felt overpowering in comparison to playing in our garden and on our street. We had also just moved house, a thing I have done frequently all my life even though I find change hard to handle. Looking back, everything about my young life feels unstable as this was the beginning of my parents splitting up.

The infant teacher, who I can 'see' in my memory but can't for the life of me name, was eager for us to grasp concepts of literacy and numeracy quickly. I took to those awful 'Janet and John' readers with ease; the family depicted was so settled and fixed, though I quickly became bored with their repetition and uninspired activities. For mathematics, we used beautiful wooden Cuisenaire® Rods – these were never boring. I felt secure and creative when I used them. I would have loved to paint not just draw them, take them outside to play, use them how they were intended by their inventor. Instead we had them for 15 minutes' addition and subtraction practice and then had to put them away.

One day, to my horror, I went to get the blocks because teacher said it was numbers time. 'You don't need those today, you can do these sums on your own, they're easy'. I have never liked mathematics at school ever since this firm, immovable instruction. I was unable to express my horror in words at that moment but it feels like ever after I stumbled and cried my way through many an hour of utterly confusing calculations being told I was stupid to whine and make such a fuss about wanting the rods which were for babies. I was never allowed to play with them again. I was seen as stupidly stubborn to keep asking.

After 55 years it was a delightful relief to touch the new version of the rods again and to think that a new generation of teachers were being encouraged to teach with them.

J. Votilla

This story is not about me as a learner before becoming a teacher, but rather as a lifelong learner in my profession. It was in my second or third year as a professional that Facebook arose, and as we now know, it created ripples across the world in terms of the publishing and sharing of personal information, and how that can impact a person's professional image. This is a story of the negative impact it can have.

When Facebook first came out it was, of course, my students who introduced me to it. Quite quickly my friends list was populated by 90 per cent students and former students. I am sure that you can see where this may be leading but in 2005, few were yet cautious about social media management and privacy. Hence, I was getting tagged all over the place in photos and events, even if I was not present in the photos, and of course nobody paid it any serious attention. Then one day I got called into my boss's office. He seemed unusually reserved, which was unnerving. He pulled out a printout of a photograph that I was tagged in, of two women kissing. 'A parent just sent me this. She asked me if this is a reflection of what our teachers' morals are like. What the hell do I say to her?' And then he just looked at me.

The photo contained two young women that were personal friends of mine, heck I even knew their families, and who were in a serious relationship at the time; but in a conservative Catholic city, this was now an issue of considerable consequence in terms of public opinion. How a mother of a current student could find such a photo was at first baffling, but the end result was a chaotic roll-out of accusations and outrage. We were eventually able to manage the situation to minimise the damage, but that was the day that I learned about the importance of social media privacy. Within a day I un-friended 200 people and explored the tiny little gear symbol on the Facebook page to control who can see what and who can tag me or post on my wall. Other teachers quickly followed suit and even created second Facebook pages for their professional lives. I changed my name on my personal account so that I could not be Googled.

Years later, at a new school, I keep my Facebook *very* private, not even allowing colleagues access to it. Recently I had a new colleague get very upset with me for not adding him, calling it a reflection of our relationship as friends. However, I stuck to my guns in the face of his constant reprimands, because never will I allow myself to get burned like that again. In hindsight, this was excellent thinking because the poor young fool, even after I had explained to him *why* I will not add any teachers to my friend list, had added 15 current students to his Facebook and ended up having his own meeting with the head of school about his own social media 'incident'.

To conclude, social media is a powerful tool that has amazing applications for teaching and learning ... but if you want to use it, then you had best create your own professional accounts and *always* keep them separated from your personal ones. Remember: kids will *always* Google you, so you had best control what they can find.

Reflections

As we read through these narratives we felt a sense of individuals in the spotlight – a spotlight which emphasised their position as an outsider at that moment in time. Whether this was Lisa visiting a strange new country and realising that her classmates saw her as 'other' or Helen and Tony being refused ways of learning that they knew deep down would allow them to be successful. It is interesting to note that for Helen and Lucy it was a teacher of mathematics who made them feel excluded from the club which had 'good at mathematics' as a condition of entry and that for Tony it was mathematics that allowed him to take control over a system he realised did not meet the needs of the learners.

This sense of exclusion, of isolation, also appears in the theme of bullying, or the abuse of power, which runs through all the narratives. There is the extreme example of Cass surviving in an ideological system designed to exclude and oppress. This is a case of state-sanctioned bullying and violence but there are also stories of teachers bullying learners. Helen and Lucy are cases in point. However, throughout these stories we can read how, on occasions, learners would take control, making teachers' lives very difficult. For example, Tony exerted some power over his infant teacher, and Ed and his peers made it their explicit aim to make teachers cry. There are also narratives in which learners exert power over other learners. Lisa's classmates in the US made sure that she was aware where the power lay when she first arrived in their classroom.

We felt that all the stories showed that the authors found ways of responding creatively to these negative experiences. Although they can be painful, there is a sense that we have used these experiences to develop a resilience. We use these experiences to explore what our values are. We can come to understand what we believe in by noticing what it is that makes us uncomfortable. We can see what justice looks like by noticing injustice.

These are stories of how we have created order out of chaos, whether that chaos was nationwide, in our childhood homes or in our educational experiences. We have determined how we can do better than those who treated us unfairly. By drawing on these negative experiences, we have worked to become the best teachers we can possibly be. As Lucy reminds us an important part of being a teacher is being an authentic human being.

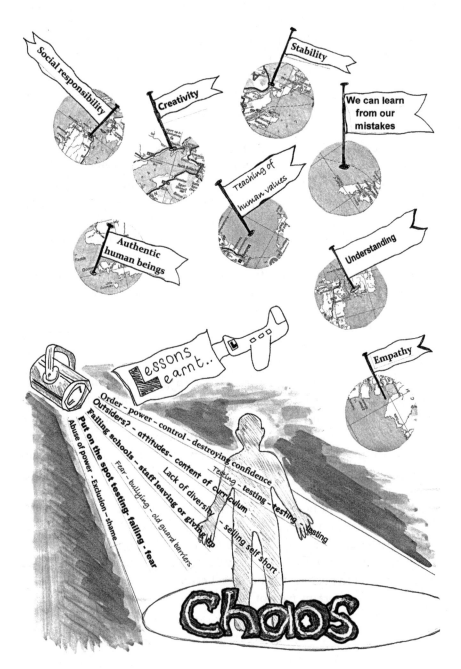

Figure 6.1 Graphical summary: Lessons learned.

Commonplace book: Entry 6

Write, in as much detail as you can, about a time when a teacher was unfair.

Reread the narrative and reflect on these questions:

• What does this incident tell you about the school?

• How did the incident make you feel?

• What would you have liked the teacher to do differently?

• What would you do now in a similar situation?

Chapter 7

Significant moments in our journeys

Chapter 6 described in some detail moments that have stayed with us throughout our lives. We acknowledged that the individuals concerned often did not deliberately set out to humiliate us and would be mortified to know that these events had remained in our memories. Similarly, the moments that we reflect on in this chapter have spoken to us across the years although the advice or support we were offered was probably forgotten in an instant by the person giving it. One of the difficulties for teachers is that we can never predict when a 'critical incident' for one of our students is taking place.

We have all been motivated to move forward in our journey in one way or another, otherwise we would not have written this book and you would not be reading it. Sometimes we want to meet ambitions others have for us, sometimes the motivation comes from our wanting to prove wrong someone who has told us we would never be successful. And sometimes we find ourselves in an institution or in a classroom that inspires us.

Some of these narratives reflect on individuals that have acted as role models or that have supported us through moments of crisis or periods of loss of confidence. Others describe a time when we thought, 'I can do this. I have the resources to move forward'.

Lucy Cooker

Perhaps it is a cliché, but those who have kept me going through some of my most trying moments as a teacher are the students themselves. In my first teaching job at a language school in Japan, it was the students who made incredible gains in communicative ability despite the dull textbook-focused lessons, a constantly changing rota of teachers and some appalling teaching practices from unqualified teachers. The students' commitment inspired me and helped me realise that learners themselves are the most powerful resource that learners have. My professional interest in learner autonomy was shaped by these early experiences. Similarly, when I was working at the University of Birmingham, and struggling to finish my PhD thesis, it was an inspirational class of students from around the world who kept me focused and excited through their motivation for learning. As well as students, one individual stands out for me, as having a formative influence on my professional journey. That is the late Dr Francis Johnson.

I had spent two years living and working in Japan, loving the teaching, but hating the language school network I was working for, when I decided to return to the UK and study for an MA so I could return to Japan and gain a better job. After a year of full-time study, I was called for an interview in a small, private university just outside Tokyo. My interview was in a hotel in London with the Director of the English Language Institute in the university, Dr Johnson. I left the interview certain that I had not been successful but to my great surprise I was offered the post and Frank became a mentor and role model for me for the next eight years of my life.

Frank was already in his late 60s when I first knew him. He worked for a Japanese university where there was a traditional system of patriarchal hierarchy and where outdated pedagogical practices were expected to be followed. Frank though was a revolutionary. He had a progressive vision for the English Language Institute that he led and was not bound by the expectations of a conventional system. Early in my time at Kanda University of International Studies, I felt energised in my teaching and empowered in my status as a female employee in ways in which I hadn't previously. Frank would always have an open door and would take time every day to check in with staff members which increased our feelings of being cared for and of belonging.

One day I went to Frank to propose an idea I had had for the development of a self-access centre within the institute. He was positive and encouraging. When I returned two weeks later with a detailed proposal for the centre, including an evidence-based rationale, measured-out floor plans, and two budgets, one for the initial set-up and the other for ongoing resourcing, he told me he would present it at the Executive Board meeting for approval later that month.

A pilot centre was approved and built and two years later our team won a significant amount of funding from the Japanese government to build a new centre and to increase our staffing. Under Frank's continued mentorship, the new centre went from strength to strength and became an example of 'best practice' in the English language teaching field in Japan. This week, 16 years on, I was notified that the university had opened a brand new centre where the exciting pedagogical developments we first put in place with the initial proposal have been given further room to develop and grow. I feel proud that Frank's belief in me as a teacher and his progressive outlook which empowered me to give free rein to my vision for our students continues to have an impact on language learning for Japanese students today.

Tony Cotton

As someone who has enjoyed working in universities I like to be able to theorise my values and beliefs rather than just see them as things plucked out of the air. Munir Fasheh, a Palestinian, Harvard PhD mathematics educator provided this during a shared inspirational moment that left a large room full of mathematics teacher educators in tears. This took place at the Mathematics Education and Society Conference in 2015 in Portland, Oregon. Munir had challenged us to think of learning and assessment through new eyes. He defined the Arabic concept of *mujaawarah* as a personal and communal freedom to learn and act in harmony with well-being and wisdom. We spent a moment thinking of how often such a freedom exists in our classrooms and how we might adapt our classrooms to act in harmony with well-being and wisdom. He also redefined assessment for us in terms of the concept of *yuhsen.* *Yuhsen,* he told us, is a combination of our performance in action and our performance in relation to our community and our environment. If we take *yuhsen* as underpinning assessment, then a person's worth is judged by assessing the interconnectivity of:

- how well they use a skill they have
- the beauty of the outcomes of using such a skill
- the usefulness of the outcomes to their community
- the respectfulness of the process
- the humility of the act.

In the previous version of this book I could not think of an individual who had inspired me. Perhaps this was because my focus was on my time as a learner in school and university. When I look back on my time in school and at university the overwhelming memory is of boredom. The stuff that I could do seemed to come effortlessly, the stuff I couldn't do, I tended to ignore. I followed a path that was expected of a good middle-class white English boy at the time. Get some O levels, follow these up with some A levels. Pick the one you are most successful in and study it at university. Then I fell into teaching, partly because I knew I didn't want to work for a big corporation. So far, so little motivation – until very recently I would have defined motivational moments for me in terms of oppositions. Opposition to someone who told me I couldn't do something, anger with someone who I felt had done me or my loved ones wrong.

However, when sitting at my writing desk I look up from the laptop, I see a bullet-pointed list on my noticeboard. I have pinned it there to remind me of what is important to me, of what motivates me. The list was constructed as an outcome of counselling I was having as I was recovering from a heart attack over six years ago. While I was somewhat sceptical about the idea of counselling I did find a weekly conversation with someone who was a good listener very helpful. The list reads:

Things that are important to me:

- valuing each other as human beings
- working together for a common purpose
- being surprised and challenged by new ideas and experiences
- working in a community not hidebound by hierarchies
- diversity which brings energy and new ideas and experiences
- people valuing what I do and finding it useful
- having somewhere safe for myself and those I love
- creating and building family traditions
- making connections between times, people and places
- open spaces.

I realise now that I learned these values from the way that we operated as a family when I was growing up. There were always fixed moments in the day, the week, the year. A family meal together at the end of the day, a Sunday day trip for a walk or a visit to friends, and, every year, a camping holiday, often involving a ferry trip, always involving an overfull green Cortina estate packed with tents, and boxes and boxes of Vesta curry. These were partly a budgetary requirement and partly the result of three boys who were fussy eaters.

I notice that the list I was offered by Munir Fasheh and my own list of values or beliefs speak to each other. Maybe this is why what Munir had to say resonated so clearly with me. It feels like I spent my early life motivated by oppositions whereas my motivation as an older man is in building communities. I am becoming less cross and better at looking at the value of my own actions rather than becoming frustrated with the actions of others. Munir finished his talk by quoting an ancient Arab poet. This statement is not above my desk but it is in my heart.

Beyond right and wrong there is a field; I will meet you there.

Edward Emmett

I had mucked up my GCSEs so couldn't do what I'd really wanted to do at college when I was 16 which was to be an accountant. I signed up for sports science at university as this was supposed to be a course that mopped up everyone who hadn't achieved well. At least it connected to my previous experience as I was football coach in my spare time. This had been my first proper paid job so I felt that a sports science course would be related to my interests and experience and be manageable academically.

As part of the course I was sent to work with two professional cricket coaches in Harrow teaching primary school children. My job was to be their assistant. They were not there to train me but just by working alongside them I realised that I did have some hope, after all, about having a career. I wouldn't just have to work in a supermarket stacking shelves. I could see myself doing what they were doing. It wasn't as if they were absolutely brilliant at it, or were bothered at all about me. It was just that I could watch professionals at work and see what a step up from my previous coaching experience could be like. My previous experience of coaching had been: collect everybody's £1; set the cones out; have a football match. This felt like proper coaching or even personal training. The coaches were giving advice, working with children inside normal school hours and teaching them to reach a higher level. This was not an after-school club designed to look after kids with nowhere else to go.

It made me realise that my footballing skills, which I hadn't been able to use to play professionally as I was not good enough, could be used to support children, or even adults, to reach their full potential. This was the first step towards me ending up becoming a teacher.

Lisa Fernandes

As part of my move from being a teaching assistant to being a homeroom teacher, I was asked by the primary principal to spend part of the week in the learning support department. There I was mentored by the P8 (Grade 5) teacher. I really looked forward to the three days I spent in P8. The teacher, backed by 20 years of experience, initially in the UK, had also worked in diverse international environments. Her highly organised, clutter-free class smelt of lemongrass that she burned every morning in a little incense burner, to give the room and the breakout space a fresh, pleasant feel. The students in her classes were always calm and purposeful. Her cheerful, clear-headed approach filtered down to the students. The lessons she planned were authentic in that they revolved around what was currently happening locally, globally and most importantly in the students' own lives. Sometimes these activities would be an inter-school football match, sometimes a school concert or a visiting author. The noticeboards were a wonderful celebration of the process and product of the students' work. The breakout space and outside area were used effectively and there seemed so much space for inquiry to take place.

The day, from the start, took on a feeling of being organised and crafted. I have often wondered how deep inquiry could take place in such a clutter-free room. Our school, in particular, is focused on integrating technology into the inquiry-based curriculum, especially in the Primary Years Programme. This teacher was so adept at using all the Google Apps for education that it was enlightening to observe her classes and watch the seamless manner in which technology was integrated with mathematics, language and the unit of inquiry modules. I realise now that by virtue of her experience, she makes her work look deceptively easy and the same task might take a new teacher like me hours to complete.

I have also fortunately had time and opportunity to observe another teacher who creates wonderful inquiry lessons, with the student at the heart of the learning. I find it so inspiring to observe these lessons and watch as this teacher guides the students to tune in and delve deeper into the concept.

These teachers seem to embody the essence of good teaching practices and the IB programme. They work at being knowledgeable, empathetic facilitators who take the responsibility of their roles very seriously. I love the idea that I work in a school which demands the use of the theory and the practice of my theoretical training. I am so pleased to be finally doing what I enjoy doing and to be mentored by experienced, creative teachers who are lifelong learners.

Han Wei

My husband has been a real mentor for me during some of my most challenging circumstances. Taking my MA was one of the most difficult things. It was a course in a second language, and it was very different from my previous understanding of academic work. One of the difficult things was to decide the topic of my assignments and my dissertation. I had to find an interesting topic I liked and to think about whether it was practical and innovative. It was always difficult to decide on the topic. I found each time that I experienced it, my husband really inspired and helped me. I also mentioned before that every time I finish teaching my husband gives me feedback.

With my assignments and dissertation there were so many topics and there were so many potentially interesting ones. I would discuss them with my husband and then when I came across a new or interesting idea he would encourage me. For example, for my technology module, I designed and explained an app for helping to learn Mandarin tones, as tones are not easy for non-tonal language speakers. So I designed it on paper and then explained it in my assignment. At the beginning I wasn't sure about this idea, as I thought there would be some different, interesting things. I told Eric about the possible topics and then told him about my idea for an app for Mandarin tones and he encouraged me to do it. He explained why he thought it was a good idea; I was a bit apprehensive because I wasn't sure if it would be really useful for people. So that's what I did and I got a distinction for my assignment.

My dissertation was torture for me! We'd done a lot of different topics and each one could have been expanded into a dissertation, so it was so hard to decide. There's an interesting topic in Mandarin, the zero pronoun, in Chinese it is common for a sentence not to require a subject. But interestingly, many second language learners don't realise it and therefore create a subject for every sentence, which sounds a bit 'English–Chinese'. The other possible topic was exploring how we can use music to teach Mandarin tones. This was very challenging because I couldn't find anyone who had done this. Teachers assume there are connections but no one had tested this or researched it. Both dissertation ideas were possible, the first was easier but the second one was more challenging, and I would also have to learn software to analyse people's speaking and to measure the pitch of the tone. I would also have to read a lot of psychology texts to understand whether we could use music to teach Mandarin tones. I knew it would be challenging to read the psychology texts!

I talked to my supervisor about both ideas and he suggested I should go for the music one. I nearly gave up even though my supervisor was encouraging. I was the last one in my class to decide my topic. I talked to Eric quite a lot about my topic and he always encouraged me and inspired me. He said:

> You gave up your job in China in order to change your career. You've developed so much, so why don't you challenge yourself and do something you really want to do? You will only have this opportunity once in your life. If you do something really good you might inspire other people, or you might continue to do further research. Have a try!

So in the end I decided to do it. Eric has played such an important role in my life and encouraged me to challenge myself. I ended up getting a distinction but I worked so hard for it! I was very happy with the results of my study.

Eric also plays an important role in my career. After working in the court in China I didn't think about changing my career. One of the reasons I did change was so that we could be together and so we discussed our circumstances and decided that it was the best thing for me to come to the UK.

I've applied to another university for a PGCE this year. It's very expensive as I don't get a bursary but Eric has said he will support me and that this is a good time for me to study. One year ago, I applied for a mathematics PGCE programme and I got a place. I was undecided whether or not I should go for it. Then Eric questioned whether I was happy to work as a mathematics teacher or whether I should stay as a Mandarin teacher. Eventually this question helped me to make the decision. Eric asks me questions and challenges me about whether I'm happy in life and whether I'm enjoying my work.

Cassius Lubisi

Because I came from a family which couldn't afford education I had to apply for bursaries. There was a bishop of the Catholic Church, Bishop

Reiteerer. He used to be the bishop of the diocese where I grew up. When I was young I was seen by him as an exemplary person. I was an exemplary altar boy and he got to know me through observing me undertake my altar boy duties. He decided that I would be able to better myself and made sure that my family had the resources to support me. He is the guy who really batted for me every time. He raised funds for me to go to Inkamana High School. He got me the place and gave me a bursary so that my family could afford the fees and buy the resources that I needed. He is also the one who first gave me a bursary to go to university. I owe Bishop Reiteerer a lot.

Haana Sandy

My motivation to succeed started from a familiarisation course at Leeds Metropolitan University (now Leeds Beckett) for teachers who had qualified outside the UK and who had been displaced from their home countries for different reasons. It was taught by Helen and opened my eyes to my new country, giving me a short taste of schools in England. It was a really good starting point for me. I got support from both Helen and Tony and now I am writing this book with them.

Another person who supported me was a deputy head teacher at the school in which I now work. Before I got the job I was a supply teacher at the school. This deputy head used to come into my lessons and she noticed how seriously I was taking my work. She was very happy with me and told me that she wanted to change my contract to permanent. She helped me a great deal with my application form. She proofread my cover letter and supported me in getting ready for interview. Even on the day of the interview she put me at ease. She boosted my confidence at every stage of the process and gave me lots of positive feedback. I will never forget her professional kindness. She was not a friend but a genuine professional guide. Knowing how to work in a system is just what I needed. She was like an angel who gave me strength to face all the pressures. She has recently become a head teacher in a newly built school for learners with special educational needs.

Helen Toft

'I've come to say I'm not going to be a teacher, I've changed my mind', I announced to my course tutor at university. I had thought about this moment all night while replaying all the challenges on my two 'teaching practices', as they were called then. I was trying to convince myself I wasn't any good at teaching even though my trainee teaching experiences were not awful at all. However, significant incidents which happened around me and over which I had no control eventually culminated in making me want to give up the idea of teaching all together. I felt powerless to change the nature of the institutions I taught in. They all seemed to have the same fault. It seemed impossible to see myself as a teacher in this system.

It wasn't the students' behaviour, although that hadn't been all plain sailing. In fact I had had fabulous moments of intense satisfaction from being creative with young people and this had encouraged me and made it seem possible that I could be a teacher. What I couldn't accept was the fact that caning, corporal punishment was being liberally used by deputy head teachers. I came to see these teachers taking the 'attack dog' role in school hierarchies during the time of my training.

My own secondary head teacher was a Quaker, so although I was at school in one of the most prolific periods of corporal punishment, it was something unknown to me. My first teaching practice was in a town in South Yorkshire in England. It felt the place that time had forgotten. Teachers chatted and developed hobbies like woodwork and knitting in the staffroom at playtime and lunchtime because they had no other duties. Lessons were mainly 'copy this off the blackboard'. The deputy head ate grapefruit for lunch, feeding the severity of her look. Some of the students smoked cigarettes from an early age and one day a group of 12-year-old girls came late to my lesson squeezing their hands under their armpits. They had been caught smoking and caned by the pinch-cheeked deputy. Would it stop them smoking, I asked in awe, to which, of course, they sneered and blustered, 'No!'

Shocked by this, but forgiving it as being Rotherham's backward-looking behaviour I happily went to my second placement in a school in Sheffield. Here I felt much more at ease. I had a young dynamic drama teacher as my mentor. I was confident I had found a possible teaching post here as the head of department was retiring and he had said a probationary job was mine if I wanted it and my mentor would step into his role – bliss!

Just days before returning to university for the final sessions before graduating, I was sitting in the staffroom on my own. I remember I was planning some risky but exciting lessons. I heard a noise I couldn't identify but went to the small window of the adjoining room to investigate and witnessed the next thwack of a cane on a boy I recognised as a bit of a challenge in my lessons. I could tell it hurt. I froze. I still wish to this day I had burst into the room but instead I went home and struggled with my conscience about entering a profession which actively supported what I consider, and still do consider, to be child abuse. That was when I decided I would not be a teacher. I went to my tutor instead of back to school the next day. My tutor at university, Bernard was shocked by my announcement. He had thought everything was going really well for me. He proceeded to try to convince me that I should be a teacher. He suggested I look at a job he had just been asked to advertise at High Green School on the outskirts of Sheffield. The school adjoined the woods in which the book *Kes* by Barry Hines had been filmed. Bernard knew the head teacher there did not agree with corporal punishment. To cut a long story short I ended up getting the job at High Green and I am so glad I did as this was the school in which the most important and formative experiences which fed my whole career happened. Caning was banned first in Sheffield schools and then the rest of the country soon after I took up this post.

J. Voytilla

When I first became a teacher, I started at a prestigious private school in Mexico. I was part of a group of 15 foreigners who were hired to teach our respective university subject areas, but in English. They piled us all together in a classroom for two weeks and ran us through some basic teacher training. When I arrived at my specific campus, I fell under the wing of my department head and a senior biology teacher, and between the two of them they pretty much shaped me into an effective and professional educator.

I must admit, I had little idea what I was doing. From my jaded experience, a teacher was the dull boring person that stood at the front of the class and waxed on and off about some facts and figures that students were obliged to note down and simply absorb with rapt attention. Again, I was an expert in naiveté and ignorance.

I was thrust into a classroom with 37 rowdy upper-class Mexican teenagers and told to teach them to somehow care about learning salient concepts such as the Kreb's cycle and electron configuration; in short, things that had zero relevance to their lives. It would be a gross understatement to say that the traditional approach to teaching such topics was rather limited in effectiveness. My classroom was absolute chaos. First off, it was completely acceptable to my students to randomly shout out to their buddies on the other side of the room, or suddenly stand up and walk around during discussions ... unless they were hungover in which case they slept at their desks. I must reiterate: I had little idea what I was doing.

My initial reaction to such behaviour was to react negatively, and of course this only exacerbated the situation and I ended up wasting 15–20 minutes of each lesson arguing with students in a feeble attempt to maintain some semblance of order. There were definitely some cultural hurdles I had yet to learn to prepare for.

After a particularly disastrous examination, my head of department Arturo called me into his office for a meeting. He heard me out, and then shared what he had heard from the students themselves, which was not particularly flattering. He suggested that I go meet with Rebeca, our senior biology teacher, to solicit her advice on classroom management. Timorously I made my way to her office and introduced myself. Almost 20 years my senior, she was a radiant sea of tranquillity and expertise who graciously took me under her wing. Her response to my initial problem on classroom management was quite frank: my dear, you need to use *your* strengths to design your classes, not someone else's.

Rebeca then made several suggestions that almost made me blush, but once I had the courage to employ them, they blew my socks off with the sudden transformation that occurred. First, I needed to act my age more. As a young teacher, quite often you tend to be preoccupied with demanding complete formal respect from the students at all times because you feel that your close age is a detriment to being seen as a professional. Second, she told me to exploit the fact that I was exotic to my students, because this would engage their personal interest, even if the lesson topic itself did not. Third, she told me to talk less and get them working more. I did not realise it at the time but she helped me to create a student-centred classroom. Thus, instead of trying to act like some stuffy and grizzled professor from yesteryear, I began to act, well, like myself. Laughing and joking with my students during class encouraged them to become interested in what was going on, because it was now fun. By getting to know my students more personally, I began to exchange life stories and experiences with them, and the students then began to care about who I was because I showed that I cared who *they* were. Sure, this ended up costing me lesson time, but it was time spent constructing relationships instead of yelling at kids to behave all the time, and it made the actual content parts of the lesson exponentially more effective.

Soon enough, kids began to say that they loved my classes, and would work hard on the material that didn't interest them, and they would even come to school the day after a big party *just for my class*, despite pounding headaches and red eyes. Soon enough students would show up at my office after class to talk about personal issues they were having, because they felt that I cared, and my foreignness meant that I wouldn't judge them the way that another Mexican might. This success encouraged me to further my own classroom innovations and design learning activities that played to my students' strengths and passions instead of trying to make them learn using someone else's. Examples include the physics of a good soccer kick from their favourite players, or the chemistry involved in making lipstick or beer. I even started playing club music all the time during class that made it seem cool to be there and work on a set of physics problems or build a model of a cell, Counter-intuitively it also kept the noise of conversation down since they wanted to hear the songs.

By teaching me to be myself and use my own strengths, Rebeca made my classes more authentic and engaging not only for my students, but also for me. Teaching was now fun! And lesson planning was exciting because it stimulated my creativity in new and innovative ways.

I must conclude with one caveat, given later to me by Arturo once he realised my turnaround success: you can be a friend to your students, but they cannot be *your* friends. At first I was saddened to hear this, but as time wore on I began to understand just how important it is to set limits on those wonderful relationships. Hence, when a group of students from my very first cohort of teaching invited me to their secret graduation fiesta in their final year, it was with great reluctance but considerable strength of will that I turned them down.

Reflections

The key theme that emerged for us when we discussed these narratives was that of belonging, of finding a home. Sometimes we needed an individual to take us by the hand and lead us into this home. This individual believed in us and knew what we needed at our particular stage of the career. Bernard took on this role for Helen and Frank for Lucy. Lisa visited a classroom in the International School in Bangalore and knew that this was 'home'. She describes the experience in vivid detail. We can tell that this memory is as vivid now as it was then. For Ed and Tony no individual had acted as a role model or mentor during their early career but they had developed a clear sense of values and this helped them decide what it was they wanted to be.

These moments are significant as they all exist on the cusp of inadequacy and empowerment. It is at times when we feel most vulnerable that we are open to taking action. These are moments when the paths of our journeys had a clear fork. But on each occasion, we knew which fork it was we had to take, whether we had a guide or whether we were journeying alone. These significant moments are also all moments when we had to draw on our core values and beliefs to make a decision. And in drawing on these core values we came to realise why our values are central to the way we operate as teachers and as human beings.

In that sense, we have all found a field that was beyond right and wrong. This has become our safe place – a place to which we can return when we need succour and encouragement; a place we return to when we need nourishment and when we have difficult decisions to make.

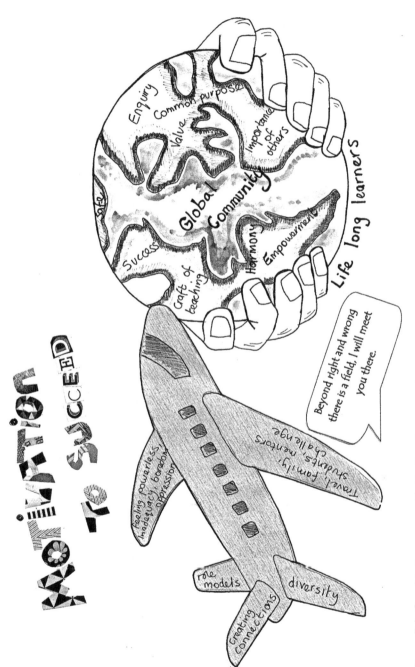

Figure 7.1 Graphical summary: Motivation to succeed.

Commonplace book: Entry 7

Can you recall a significant moment in your education journey?

Is there an individual who has acted as a mentor or a role model for you?

Is there an individual who inspires you to 'be like them'?

Is there an institution that embodies your personal educational beliefs?

Part 3

Our experiences as teachers

So far the narratives in the book have focused on our experiences in education as learners. And deliberately so. These experiences are not insignificant and are formative in many different ways. The time we have spent in education as a learner will have a huge impact on us when, to some extent, we switch roles, and become teachers. It is no surprise that beginning teachers often feel closer to the learners they are working with than their new colleagues. I remember feeling slightly odd the first time I entered a staffroom without having to knock on the door. There was a kind of sense of changing sides. Having said all of this it is also important to explore our experiences in education as teachers.

This structure is deliberate. There is a difference between reflecting on our experiences as learners and using these experiences to inform our teaching, and observing others teach and drawing on this to inform our practice. In some ways, it is more difficult to learn from others than it is to learn from ourselves. We cannot simply repeat what seems to work for other people, in the same way that we cannot endlessly repeat one-off lessons that went particularly well. Teaching is much more complicated than that. What we need to attempt is to turn other people's good practice into our own good practice so that, in some sense, we embody that practice. When this happens, people will observe us and think that it is our practice, not someone else's that we are copying. And, ultimately, we will get to the stage when we have forgotten that we teach in this way because we drew on inspiration from someone else.

Before we can learn from other teachers and even before we can notice what is successful in our own practice we need to 'learn' how to observe teaching and learning. This is incredibly difficult at first. At the end of a year-long course a beginning teacher once said to me, 'I have only just learned how to observe well. If I had known this at the beginning of the year everything would have been so much simpler'. However, this did not mean that the year had been wasted, rather that the skill of observation takes a while to master. In one of the stories that follows, Lucy writes about the importance of knowing what you are looking for when observing others, of co-constructing an observation pro forma so that discussion after an observation can be tightly focused on particular pedagogical approaches.

The narratives that follow offer you views from many different classrooms, in many different contexts. Some will feel comfortable for you, some might feel strange. We hope that some of the stories will make you wonder what you can learn and take into your practice as a teacher. What you can adapt and use in your own context. Within this part, you will find a whole range of teaching approaches and styles. Perhaps simply seeing the different possibilities available to you may help you think through your own preferred teaching style.

Chapter 8

Watching others teach

Watching others teach is an important part of professional development at all levels. As beginning teachers, we observe others in order to learn the basic skills of our craft; we might observe others or invite observations as part of an in-service professional development programme; experienced teachers and leaders might observe beginning teachers or experienced teachers in order to provide an opportunity for reflective practice and to offer feedback.

Teachers do not have enough time to watch others teach. One of the best ways to share what has come to be termed as 'best practice' is surely to watch this practice in action. So, our memories of great lessons we have seen are invaluable. It allows us to reflect on what it was about that particular lesson that had fixed it in our memory over other lessons we will have observed; what attaches the definition of 'best practice' to that lesson, at least in terms of our own values and beliefs. These observations also invite us to reflect on how we would adapt and develop the lesson for our own subject area or for the learners we are working with. What would we do the same, what would we change, what do we think we couldn't attempt at all?

It was interesting that two of the co-authors of this book found it very difficult to think of observations of others that had inspired them. In the UK at the moment there is a focus on observation to make judgements on people rather than on observation for mutual professional development. We hope that the stories that follow allow you to access some of the power that can come through collaborative observation.

Lucy Cooker

I started my teaching career as an English language teacher by taking a four-week Teaching English as a Foreign Language to Adults (TEFLA) course. I remember the day I went for my interview to be accepted onto the course at Bell Language Schools' Bowthorpe Hall. I told Alan, my interviewer, that I was thinking I might one day go into mainstream teaching. He responded by saying that English teaching is a great start to a mainstream teaching career as you can take a lot of the good practice from English language teaching (ELT) into mainstream schools, but it's harder to transfer the practice in the other direction.

The four weeks of the course were a wonderful experience for me. The Cambridge TEFLA course was known for the large number of lesson observations, micro-teaching and teaching sessions that take place from the first day. I loved watching classes being taught and lessons being crafted in front of my eyes. As student teachers, we would have time to familiarise ourselves with the lesson we would be observing later that day, then we would observe the lesson in groups of three or four. The lessons were short, usually 35 minutes. We would look for a particular piece of teaching practice. For example, the amount of 'teacher talking time' (at that time, one feature of communicative language teaching was to minimise the amount of time a teacher talks in order to maximise the amount of time that students are talking). We would take notes and use these later to discuss and reflect upon the lesson. The teachers we observed seemed masterful. They skilfully made their points clear, using English to communicate even when the students understood very little of the target language. Small-group work was employed regularly for different activities throughout one lesson to maximise communication opportunities at a level of language that was accessible for everyone. 'Realia', real objects, were utilised to aid understanding and activities were pitched at different levels for different abilities with additional work available for those who finished early. Sometimes this additional work would take the form of helping others in the class. Now I can identify how these practices are just a part of good teaching, but at the time they felt very far away from the practices I had been exposed to as a student in school in the 1970s and 1980s. It was exciting to see how engaging the language students found these lessons.

Later in my career observation was an important tool for supporting the development of less experienced colleagues. I have already talked about working at Kanda University of International Studies. During my time there it was part of my role to observe my colleagues working in the self-access learning centre as learning advisors (LAs). These observations were part of an annual review and aimed to help LAs develop away from classroom teaching towards advising on effective learning.

Language advising is quite a different role from teaching in some ways, and it was fascinating to observe these sessions. As the LA role was new and innovative, we had co-constructed the criteria for observation based on an academic paper about the skills learning advisors need to develop in order to do their job. Many of these skills were taken from the field of counselling and included listening, understanding, negotiation, conflict and confirmation. The main guiding principle was that learners needed to analyse their own learning needs and make their own choices regarding materials and goals, and be guided in those by the learning advisor, rather than being told explicitly what to do and how to do it. The empowering nature of the learning advisory role meant that the observation process had to be similarly empowering, so I used verbal vignettes to describe what I had observed, and encouraged my colleagues to reflect on their own performance through these.

Tony Cotton

Rather than describing a single lesson I want to describe a recent workshop that I attended in which a primary mathematics coordinator described how she was transforming the mathematics experience of the learners in the school in which she works. She was drawing on the work of Caleb Gattegno, an Egyptian mathematician who popularised the use of Cuisenaire® Rods in the 1950s and 1960s. Helen mentioned these rods in Chapter 6. Gattegno argued that 'Only awareness is educable' (Mason 1987) and suggested that teaching should be subordinated to learning, with the teacher's role to plan activities for the learner. These activities would allow them to become aware there is something new to be learned.

The school was drawing on textbooks that Gattegno had written many years earlier, adapting these for use in their classrooms and using a curriculum map he had produced which showed how a large portion of the mathematics curriculum can be taught using these rods. The workshop opened with a very brief context setting, as I have opened this vignette. We were then given our own set of Cuisenaire® Rods and invited to have 10 minutes' 'free play' with our newly acquired rods. I noticed that each set had a name on the front. I seemed to have Ishmael's set. The workshop leader told me that she had borrowed these sets from the children in her class and that all the children were delighted they would be able to lend their set to some teachers who were learning about the sort

Figure 8.1 Cuisenaire® Rods.

of mathematics they did at their school. I became aware of how constricted I was feeling and that I was simply revisiting earlier activities with rods. Then I noticed a colleague engaged in exploration. I asked what they were doing and eagerly joined in their investigation to find out how many different ways I could arrange two or more smaller rods to make one of the larger ones.

At the end of our free-play time, time that went far too quickly, we were told that as each child enters Year 1 (age 7+) they are given their own set of rods which they are told will have to last them the six years they are at school. They carefully remove the cellophane wrapping and write their name on their rods. They then spend all the mathematics lessons in their first week on 'free play', exploring the rods, and the patterns that they make for themselves. From then on, every mathematics lesson starts with 10 minutes' free play. This is something Cattegno insisted on. He argued that it is through play that we become aware of the possibilities for learning.

We were then invited to work in pairs on a series of activities that the learners in the school had been engaged with. And we were invited to make notes on things that we became aware of as we worked on the activities. In this sense, we were invited to take note of our own growing awareness.

What is it about this workshop that makes it stand out for me? That ranks it in some way as 'best'? Let me explore my awarenesses. First, the workshop was based on a well thought through and passionately argued theory of learning. There was expertise in the room and there was commitment to a belief about learning and teaching. Second, we were invited to engage in the same activity as the learner – not to mimic what a 7-year-old might do but to see how all learners can be offered a similar starting point and develop in different ways. Third, we were invited to engage in our learning journeys collaboratively. Perhaps most importantly, the workshop, or the lesson, modelled the theory in practice. This is sometimes called 'praxis', the act of embodying a theory in practice.

I also reflected on what it might be like to be a mathematics learner in this teacher's classroom. I would be valued. I would be given a beautiful set of manipulatives that were mine to care for, for the whole of my time in school. Learning was seen as a long-term endeavour. Why else would I be given equipment on my first day that was to last for six years? And learning was collaborative and cooperative. I would learn from my teachers and would learn alongside my teachers and my peers. And finally, I would be in control of my learning, my learning was my responsibility. It was my teacher's responsibility to provide me with situations in which I could learn.

Almost as an afterthought the workshop leader told us that the learners' attainment in mathematics is improving, her colleague's enthusiasm for mathematics is growing and the whole school is now committed to this approach and believes in it.

Edward Emmett

I haven't actually observed this person formally teach, but my deputy head teacher has really built up the new secondary school that the children I teach will attend when they get older. He started at the school two years ago and the children really respect him and he really respects them, they are always talking about him. His role is sports deputy head in charge of sports development including swimming. At first, he taught Year 8 but he hasn't got time now because his inspirational sport teaching has led to so many events to organise. He's had a real influence on me and made me remember that as an adult you remember that you played in the team, not if you won or the contribution you made. It is the memory that you were selected to play and then actually played that you take with you into adulthood.

He has introduced sports at tournament level to a school which previously never took part in any activities outside the school; now we regularly play volleyball, basketball and football. He is softly spoken but gains respect from the students. He understands secondary-aged students, seems to have natural empathy with them. I have seen him with the students at events and at lunchtimes. When he is teaching volleyball for example he breaks everything down carefully. All his instructions are given in small stages. He corrects mistakes as you go and he cares a lot about technique.

He asked me to coach a football team and we began to work together by having meetings about his philosophy. He sees school sports as about 'participation and enjoyment' not simply winning. A great outcome of this approach is that we are winning. He has changed the philosophy and plans for the school development. We will be a 'sports-focused school' by the time the new head teacher is appointed in a month's time. He contacts other schools and sets up competitions carefully to ensure the other teams are partners, and that they are equally matched. This means it will be a really competitive experience.

I don't know much about his background, but think he was a wrestler at university at a very high level. He is that stocky, strong type of person. I think he will make a fantastic head teacher.

Lisa Fernandes

It is here in the IB school where I now teach that I first saw and experienced wonderful teaching methods. I was assistant to the P6 teacher and watched with joy the process of teaching through inquiry, as it unfolded. The development of skills and deepening of understanding, through lessons that were authentic, significant, relevant and challenging, were a thrill to watch. Vygotsky's constructivist theory which I had read so much about was suddenly coming alive. Prior knowledge was assessed and differentiated through hands-on activities and reflections. The learner was valued and listened to. The skills needed in concept-based learning were developed – the skills to make connections, develop a wide perspective and a positive attitude as well as taking personal responsibility to develop our own learning. It is like a breath of fresh air to watch a highly experienced practitioner deliver a high-quality lesson. I am enjoying this new burst of learning in my life.

One of the lessons I helped plan, and observed the execution of, was for the trans-disciplinary unit, 'Sharing the Planet', in Grade 3. The central idea was that water is a limited resource and needs to be conserved for the sustainability of the planet. We visited a local village and saw first-hand how precious water was; how it was stored and the conservation measures that were in place. Each student had to then find a particular local or global water issue and add it to the map we created. In pairs students had to choose an issue, research it from given resources and web links and create presentation slides exploring the issue as part of their summative task. This was then presented at the primary assembly to the whole school. The activities planned and taught during this unit developed presentation skills, teamwork and interest in global issues, and deepened the students' understanding of the world we live in.

As teachers, we have the responsibility to nurture curiosity and encourage a thirst for learning. What a joy to celebrate our students' questions and wonderings and guide them to seek their own answers. As I continue to observe and be mentored by this teacher, I have finally found what I want to be doing for the rest of my life, as a lifelong learner.

Cassius Lubisi

For me a great teacher is one who creates the conditions for one to learn independently without necessarily being forced to follow the traditions of teaching. One who will let you discover. One who takes you on a journey of discovery. For me that is a great teacher. Not someone who wants you to mimic a book or churn out what they are telling you. In that sense, I have had some truly great teachers; Sister Dorothea who I have mentioned was really and truly able to teach the structures of mathematics, the theorems and the formulae while allowing for greater experiences of discovery that were not necessarily in the curriculum at the time. This allowed us to be creative in mathematics, not only driven by examinations.

Also, a great teacher teaches by doing; they are a role model – someone who teaches through the hidden curriculum without necessarily being overt; but if you see them doing certain things and you realise that what they are doing is good you want to follow in their footsteps. I think these teachers are leaders, and that they see their role as developing leaders. As a member of the Mass Democratic Movement I have had many teachers like that. Despite their age and experience they would talk to you as a comrade. They would allow you to engage on an equal footing and express your ideas without fear. They would allow you to take risks with what you are saying. For me that is extremely good. The late Themba Harry Gwala was an absolutely amazing teacher. He was a teacher by profession but he left teaching to protest about the teaching methodology and content he was expected to follow. He was expected to tell students, 'you should every day have an egg and a glass of milk, two slices of bread and an apple'. He knew that as he couldn't afford to buy these things that he would be telling working-class black children a lie as they could not afford to buy these things either. He was expected to tell students to leave their windows open to allow air to circulate but he knew that this would mean that mosquitos would come in and spread disease.

When the apartheid education system came in he protested and started attending the national classes of the communist party that taught Marxism and Leninism. Then he started opening up political classes. He was imprisoned on Robben Island for ten years and then the second time for life. He became the political educator on Robben Island, so when many of the leaders of the ANC were imprisoned on Robben Island he introduced the 'great man' version of history. They would study history from a historical materialism perspective starting from the history of the struggles that existed at particular times.

Haana Sandy

When a new head teacher arrived at my current school he felt he needed to put 45 of his staff on a programme to develop their teaching skills. As part of that process I was given a mentor who was a geography teacher. He put me at ease about the programme. He said not to worry about it at all, just be myself, and agreed that the head was just trying to prove to government inspectors he had improved his staff as soon as he arrived at the school. We were quite cynical about the programme but not of one another. This teacher reassured me I was already a good teacher and invited me in to observe his lessons to see if there were any ideas I could use in my own classroom. The way he approached any misbehaviour was always to remain calm, he never shouted. He was gentle, fair and consistent in his teaching style. He never panicked, just stayed in control, and told me to always look as if you were in control even if underneath you were not sure.

In his lessons, he was very clear about his expectations and followed them through. If anyone was not working we were supposed to give them a 'verbal warning', but he just quietly wrote their name on the board and carried on teaching. The students noticed their name and worked hard to have their name rubbed off the board. This little twist in the school's behaviour policy really helped in my lessons because it was much less confrontational and as a busy teacher you didn't forget if you had aready given one warning.

Helen Toft

I have talked earlier in the book about an intergenerational community choir I attend and offer support to. This is a new and delightful experience for me – to be placed in the position of learner with little responsibility for the session. At first I had set out a circle as I would for a drama class but now set the room in the way suggested by one of our members who has recently passed away. The choir leader Nik and I work alongside Ann, a representative of a local charity which supports elderly people to lead active, sociable lives. The choir has become an important group for us all, and it really struck me one morning that I was learning with and from an intergenerational community of lifelong learners. We were being led by an untrained, fast developing and intuitive young teacher.

The week before, we had been struggling with a particular song, really struggling, to the extent that there was mumbling and resistance in the choir. These people are not quitters. Their determination to stay actively involved with life despite the ravages of ageing is testimony to that. But on this occasion we were far out of our comfort zones, the harmony was strange, the style unfamiliar.

Nik seems to have an instinctive understanding of the need for scaffolding and pushing learners just beyond what they thought they were capable of. He said later when I asked his permission to write this piece that he has learned it from working with a team of music teachers with some of the most socially and educationally disadvantaged children at a Saturday morning music club he founded. I think he might also have learned it from the way he was taught music, and knowing his mum a little, from her too.

The warm-ups we are asked to do in preparation for singing without damaging our throats or confidence are not always related to the song we are going to sing, but today it became obvious that Nik had found a way to break the deadlock in our enthusiasm for learning this particular song. We found that we could make sense of the demands of the tune if we followed his cue to sing our song in the style of a familiar nursery rhyme. When he combined this with asking us to follow his hand movements up and down to mark the pitch of the note and to listen carefully to the resonance left by the top note of a strummed chord (which is the one that our ear always picks out, he told us) we made progress. On reflection I think that in bringing Nik's unfamiliar new arrangement to life we were being asked to:

- open ourselves up to an experience we found uncomfortable
- utilise the musical equivalent of 'muscle memory' from our childhoods
- watch the notes of the song being 'signed'
- listen to the residual pitch of a note along with
- engaging fully with the playful approach to singing as if a small child with a rhyme.

Nik drew a picture in all our imaginations that we could and would smash through the block to our learning. Of course we did and the session ended with spontaneous applause.

As I have mentioned earlier in the book I travel from the choir to drive over to take care of our grandson. On this occasion I found myself singing with gusto in the car with my mum, aged 85, who also attends the choir. As we picked him up from his nursery he asked for a particular song on his current favourite CD and sang it word and almost pitch perfect to the delight of all.

J. Voytilla

I am going to describe the craziest class that I ever observed, and possibly the most fun that I have ever had inside my own four-walled classroom as a result. My boss in Mexico, Arturo, was renowned as an educational maverick and is a true renaissance man. He was an engineer and a hacker who could cover any class in his department, was always, and still is to this day, pushing traditional boundaries and innovating curriculum. He had created a new course called Introduction to Robotics, which was part basic civil engineering principles mixed with using Lego Robotics kits to teach the somewhat lost art (in high school at least) of hands-on learning and project management.

Due to my rising popularity with the student body, he asked me to teach the same class but in English. This was an exciting and terrifying invitation because what the hell did I know about either engineering or robotics? He looked me in the eye when I confessed this and said, 'So what. It's super fun and you will love it!' Still doubtful I accepted an offer to observe some of his classes to get the gist of how it flowed. This was to be my first introduction to problem-based learning.

His class was a beautiful representation of organised chaos. It was a class of 40+ students, working together in small groups to solve robotic and construction challenges, each group creating their own individual solutions and employing the design cycle to eventually achieve success. I had no idea what that meant at first, but for some reason *his* crazy seemed to match my own crazy and aside from the challenge of having to learn and understand elements of construction, bridge building for example, and basic programming, his class was heaven. Actually it was not really a 'class' but more of a workshop, just like Leonardo's. Following him around the room as he made his rounds from group to group, helping teams troubleshoot technical issues, personality issues, time-management issues, and bizarre logistical issues was for me more than just an eye opener to what high school education could really become; I can confidently say that it metamorphosed my perception of the learning–teaching dynamic – which I discovered in my later educational studies was called contingent teaching.

After two or three observations, I was hooked. My own workshop became some sort of crazed beast of innovation, with electronic music blaring over the speakers, while the film *Baraka* played silently on the classroom screen just to provide a sensory juxtaposition to the realm of motors and gears that the students were sweating over each day. One day our school director walked in to my workshop, and I could see instant confusion and dismay on her face. However, after observing for about five minutes, I could see her facial expression change to a small satisfied smile – she didn't even ask me to close the door as she left the noisy creativity fest. Each new robotic challenge that Arturo and I devised together provided new opportunities for inter-class collaboration and cooperation, and expanded not only my students' minds, but constantly kept blowing my hair back with the creativity that students are capable of ... if, instead of confining them to a rigid set of parameters, you unleash them. That is now one of my favourite words to use in education, and to this day I strive to unleash my students in any subject rather than confine their thinking to what they already know. I have continued Arturo's legacy in my new school as well, using Lego Robotics to teach students about creative design thinking and collaborative project management, two skills that I know will help every single one of them in whatever field their life paths take them.

Han Wei

I'm going to talk about four inspiring teachers I've encountered in my roles as a Chinese language teacher and beginning school teacher.

The first inspiring lesson is an online teaching video. It's popular in America. The first time I saw this was in the UK because of the 'firewall' issue in China in the first semester of my Masters. I was doing research about Mandarin tones online and came across it that way. The teacher's name is Yoyo Chen. Why are her videos so popular? She connected the Mandarin tones to English. We have four tones. For some non-tonal language speakers it's very hard to recognise the differences but she helped English speakers by associating them with English. For example, Yoyo found that the intonation of the part 'may' of 'maybe' is similar to the first tone in Mandarin and the intonations of the questions of 'what' 'Yeah' are the same as the second tone in Mandarin. We tried this method with our voluntary class and we found that students really liked it. And it was this that inspired me to explore Mandarin tones with music in my Masters dissertation as we can perhaps find the exact music notes to match the four Mandarin tones. It can be more interesting.

The second inspiring lesson I've observed is a mathematics lesson at a secondary school in Manchester. I observed a Year 7 mathematics class. It was about 'reflection' and 'symmetry'. The focus of the lesson was on traffic signs: roundabout signs, no-entry signs, signs indicating traffic lights, and so on. The teacher had drawn symmetry lines and reflection lines on the road signs, as traffic signs have these features of reflection and symmetry. In addition they are colourful and they also have interesting features such as arrows; this makes the activity more challenging and provides an easy way to differentiate between simple and hard tasks. After presenting the information on PowerPoint, he made small cut-out versions of all the traffic signs and then gave these to each group to allow them to explore the concepts further. It was interesting because he used real-life objects to help students understand mathematical concepts. And later, when students see those traffic signs in the world, it will remind them of reflection and symmetry.

My third inspiring lesson is also an observation of a mathematics class in a grammar school close to where I live. The way the teacher taught was not really teaching. She led the class and questioned the students about the features of the mathematics. Then she asked questions about what they had found. The whole lesson was full of questions. It was a well-designed lesson because the questions were related to the main content. She had students observe input about units (kilos, kilometres) on a PowerPoint presentation and then she asked questions. I always thought that this was a way to teach university students, but it worked for secondary students too. I had never seen questioning and demonstrations used before in this way.

The fourth one is from a conference I attended in London about Mandarin teaching. The teacher used proper rap to teach students. It was very, very innovative and I was so impressed. She used a few words – five words – and she wrote them down. The words should be the target vocabulary. She gave each group five words and asked each group to use a certain pattern for the sentence, for example 'I like noodles because ...' and then to say it in rap. By rapping and saying the words, the Mandarin tones are retained. But of course it also helps not just with sentence patterns and vocabulary, but also reading, writing and listening, so all four skills are used. She showed some of her students on video and it was so effective. The students were very creative. It was very cool – the students chose their own music and could write their own lyrics.

Reflections

As we read through these stories we were struck by common themes that cut across stories from different countries and from different disciplines. Whatever lesson was being described there seemed to be a sense of mutual respect in the learning environment – a respect between teachers and a mutual respect between learners and teachers. In school settings, this was described overtly and it could be sensed in the descriptions of teachers as softly spoken, as not having to shout; in teachers being seen to be fair and consistent. Of course, when we think about informal settings such as Helen's intergenerational choir we would not expect a teacher to shout, so why might we see this in formal education? It is always worth asking the question would the learners turn up for these lessons if it wasn't compulsory?

There was also a common thread of learners taking responsibility for their own learning, whether this was Lucy's story about the shift from teachers to LAs, and how they drew on counselling skills to develop as LAs to Tony's description of Gattegno's approach to learning and teaching mathematics. Expecting learners to take on the responsibility for their learning involves working collaboratively, being part of a team. Such collaborative work is at the heart of Lisa's and Ed's stories.

Han and Lucy, in particular, describe the ways in which teachers skilfully linked new knowledge to the lived experience of their learners. There was a sense of authenticity in the activities in which learners were engaged and Han described how, if we use traffic signs to learn about symmetry, every time we see a traffic sign we revisit that particular piece of knowledge. In this way learning mathematics changes the way that we view and experience the world.

All the teachers described here raised the bar in terms of expectations. These teachers opened up learning to people who may have been previously nervous. You have read about older people challenged by a difficult song and pupils taking part in sport at a high level, something that they might not have felt was possible. And on both of these occasions there was a shared excitement in the success.

Many of the stories are underpinned by educational theory; they are examples of theory in practice in the classroom. This is perhaps particularly true of the stories from Ed, Helen, Lucy and Tony. Here teaching is seen as a craft, and the teachers we observe are seen to be masters of this craft. We have trust in these teachers' expertise and can find things to take away from our observations. Sometimes there is surprise in a little twist to something that happens every day. Haana's story is an example of this and sometimes it is a more overarching idea, as with Ed's story of the teacher who cares about technique and makes sure that any issues are corrected immediately.

One thing that doesn't seem to ever leave us is a sense of playfulness. These are stories of lifelong learning, of learning as a 'deep and long-term endeavour', as Tony puts it. Maybe we will know if we are doing it right if we can offer an 'education that is full of questions'.

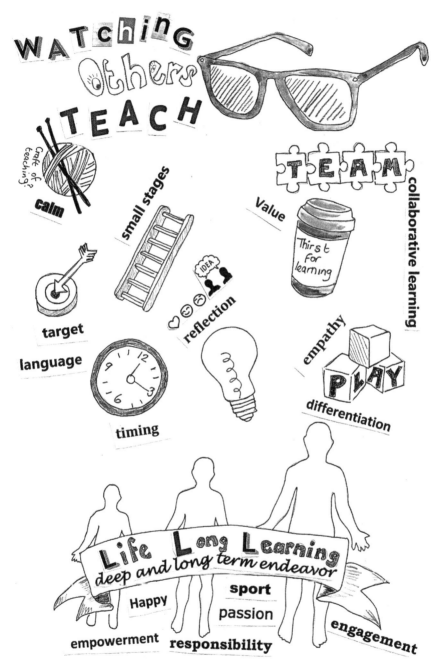

Figure 8.2 Graphical summary: Watching others teach.

Commonplace book: Entry 8

Who is the best teacher you have ever observed? Think about a particular teaching episode and write about it in as much detail as you can.

What makes this the 'best' lesson you have ever seen? What makes it different from all the other lessons you have watched?

What did you learn as a result of this observation? How have you changed your approach?

Chapter 9

Our best lessons

Introduction

Our own best lessons didn't appear out of thin air and nothing that we do is original. I would actually argue that we shouldn't feel the need to be original. Our own best lessons will develop out of the best lessons that we have observed. This is why Chapter 8 is important. And why the order of these two chapters is important. What is original is the use of the idea, or the strategy, or the resource in a new setting, with a new group of learners and to use it effectively. And, of course, the idea will be new to every new group that we use it with.

There is always much discussion in the school effectiveness and school improvement literature about the importance of string leadership and management – about how string leadership can turn failing schools around. This chapter takes the view that individual teachers make a difference to individual learners' lives.

Lucy Cooker

I'm not going to talk about my best lesson but my best course of lessons. When I worked at Kanda University of International Studies in Japan we were able to bid for the opportunity to design our own elective course for the junior and senior years (the oldest and most proficient students). As an experienced teacher, I was excited at the opportunity of designing my own curriculum and to use this experience to enable me to enact some of the principles about language learning that form part of my personal philosophy of learning. I was very interested in the use of an immersive approach to language learning, using film and television to engage and interest learners.

I designed a course called 'Language through Soap Opera' which used the long-running British television series, *EastEnders*, as the content for the course.

The term 'soap opera' describes a serial drama, usually long-running, with a focus on stories of the day-to-day lives of the characters. There are different kinds of soap operas. *EastEnders* is an example of a social realist soap opera, which means that characters are involved in storylines about relationship problems, financial hardships and petty crime; viewers are often hooked on the melodrama through a sense of relief that their lives aren't quite as desperate as those of the characters in the soap. This is in contrast to a 'glamour' soap opera in which viewers become hooked through a sense of aspiration that one day their lives might be as good as those depicted in the drama.

I selected three episodes of *EastEnders* to use in the class. These three episodes were particularly dramatic, and ended with a big fight between some of the main protagonists. Each 30-minute episode was divided up into three 10-minute sections and we worked with one section each week. My students learned about the characters, their habits, the setting (a small square in an area of East London) and the culture – both the local culture of the London context, but also the wider culture of the UK. I provided transcripts of the scenes which my students then used to analyse the language. This was a fascinating experience for my students as it gave them an opportunity to engage with 'real' conversational English. However fake the language of a soap opera character might be, it is assuredly more 'natural' than that used by the faceless characters in language textbooks. Spending time on listening to the video of East-Enders enabled my students to practise listening to language as spoken in the real world – fast speech, in which words are swallowed and not always clearly enunciated, and speakers interrupt each other leaving unfinished sentences.

Each lesson would start with watching the video. We would watch the section from the previous lesson as a short review, and then watch that week's section. After the first few lessons, the students had become familiar with the characters and were keen to know how the storyline developed. Motivation for engaging with the language was built into the very content of the lesson. Once they had watched the relevant section, I put them into groups (I would usually put them into groups according to some criteria that I changed each week – such as distance travelled from home to university, or number of buttons on their clothes – to avoid students working with the same individuals week after week). They were then asked to talk about the video and figure out what was going on. These classes were all of English medium instruction, so all these discussions took place in English. After plenary feedback on their discussions and the developing storyline, I would distribute the transcript of the scenes. Students would then identify unknown vocabulary, and talk to each other and use available resources to figure out the meaning. I would then ask them for specific vocabulary items to focus on as a group.

EastEnders is based in East London, where a form of slang called cockney is used. Sometimes we would learn cockney rhyming slang, and I would teach my students the meanings. For example, in cockney rhyming slang the word 'stairs' is replaced with the phrase 'apples and pears' so I would teach my students phrases such as 'I'm going up the apples and pears to bed'. A language form closely related to cockney is known as 'estuary English' and I would also teach my students how to use estuary English pronunciation, such as replacing the middle 't' sound with a glottal stop – so the word 'better' comes out as 'be'er'. We had a lot of fun playing with language in these ways. I used some traditional language teaching techniques from the behaviourist tradition, such as 'drilling' and 'listen and repeat' to help them master these strange aspects of the language. Normally I would resist using such techniques, as my personal philosophy of language learning is much more on communicative importance than accuracy of pronunciation, but it felt radical and almost subversive to drill students saying 'foo'baw' instead of 'football'.

Once we had learned some of these vocabulary items they would create mini role plays and conversations in which they would use these items and I would circulate in the class answering questions about grammatical structures, or some cultural aspects from the TV show that they were wondering about. In the last few minutes of the lesson I would ask them to predict what would happen in the next 10-minute section. This allowed them to draw upon their developing understanding of the characters, the culture and the language, and to use their imaginations to come up with some exciting melodramatic moments of their own creation.

I loved teaching this course, and my students loved the lessons. It was always the most popular elective class in the year. I often wonder whether the legacy of my time in Japan is an increased use of glottal stops in the spoken English of a small group of Japanese people living just outside Tokyo.

Tony Cotton

I find it difficult to pick out what might be my own best lesson. How do I know? Surely our best lessons are defined by the response of those we are teaching. And the problem with teaching is that we never really know the impact that our lessons will have on our learners. Of course, our learners don't know the impact either, not until much later. John Mason, one of my gurus, if we are allowed such a thing, once said, 'Teaching takes place in time, learning takes place over time'. If this is indeed the case, we have no way of knowing if lessons have been successful or not.

However, I can share the most moving piece of feedback I ever received from a student in one of my 'lessons' and share with you thoughts as to why what I had been doing might have led to this feedback.

I had been teaching a group of 24 beginning teachers on a summer school. They had all been placed in schools for one week and had attended a day's induction into mathematics education at a university. I had two and a half days with them. They would then be placed in the primary school in which they were going to work and to some extent be expected to learn on the job. This felt like a big ask so I had thought very carefully about exactly what I might consider absolutely vital to cover. Sometimes the expectation to be concise focuses the mind.

At the end of the final session I found a post-it note stuck to my planning notes on the desk at the front. The note read,

> Bits were difficult and scary as my disability has left me with very little working memory
>
> But . . .
>
> You are the first teacher who has ever made me feel confident about employing creative strategies in teaching and solving maths problems.
>
> Thankyou ☺

To this day, I don't know who this student was. I didn't know that any of the group had a disability although I did know that some of the group were challenged by what I was asking them to do and that they will have found this a bit scary. I thought back over what I had worked on – I always start by asking all participants to engage in some form of people mathematics, and this is always an activity which allows the participants to get to know each other and which tries to foster a sense of community and trust within and across the group. On this occasion, the group were finding people who satisfied certain conditions: someone with the same number of siblings; someone who had travelled further than them to reach the seminar; someone whose house number shared a property with theirs; someone who could count to 20 in languages other than English; and so on. After a debrief in which we discussed the benefits of multilingualism in particular and diversity in general for mathematics teaching, the complexity contained in a question as simple as 'how many siblings do you have?' and that shared property can always be found between two numbers, we moved on to engage in a piece of mathematics that they might recognise from school. Today I asked the group to complete a multiplication square (see Table 9.1).

At this point, many in the group defaulted into solitary working although I hadn't asked them to work alone. For some this brought about feelings of inadequacy or lack of confidence in their recall of multiplication facts. While most will try to work systematically through the grid, as that is the method they recall from school (and are immediately confronted by 8 × 7) there is always someone who will see that they could start by multiplying by 10 and halving these answers to find the 5s column. Similarly, we could start with the 2s row, double these to find the 4s, double again to find 8s and so on. Through this discussion, I redefine mathematics as something that we all do together and something that is achievable for all. A good mathematician, I suggest, is someone who uses what they know to work out what they don't know. We will also explore our feelings about learning mathematics and think through how these are formed by our previous experiences as learners. Most importantly we work on ways that we can support our learners into having a positive view of themselves as learners of mathematics.

Table 9.1 A multiplication grid

X	7	5	1/2	1/4	10
8					
4					
3					
2					
6					

I think that learners in school classrooms best learn mathematics in groups where diversity of prior experience is valued and different prior experience is seen as beneficial rather than a hindrance. So that is what I model in the mathematics we work on together. I don't tell beginning teachers how to teach mathematics – I teach them mathematics, at their own level, so that they can feel what it is to learn and to teach mathematics. And, at least on this occasion, it appears to have worked.

Edward Emmett

It is a series of lessons I want to talk about. I have taught them every year since I started teaching but in 2016 it was so successful that I repeated it in 2017. I was away from school critically ill for the actual event so didn't see it happen this year. We follow the English Early Years Foundation Stage framework but the final project of this curriculum is 'Castles' which is not relevant to Thai children. So, instead, I focus on the community and invite parents to come in and lead a session on their culture and expertise. This also links with a celebration of 'International Day' which I make into a big event to celebrate all the different cultural backgrounds of the children in my class.

I taught the class exploring English culture which was fine but not out of the ordinary. Another teacher who is South African taught about her culture and an Australian mother came in to teach about hers. Five Korean mothers led a session too but by far the most exciting and important session was the classroom of 100 Thai parents, 52 students and their younger siblings. This was chaotic but brilliant. I don't speak Thai so all the planning with the parents was through my Thai teaching assistant. The presentation was supposed to start at 9am with a 10-minute introduction, followed by a song and dance for ten minutes and then some discussion about costume and food in Thailand. The session was supposed to last 45 minutes in total. What actually happened was that we began at 9.45am because so many parents had arrived and then the session went on for three hours. We had to cancel break and the Chinese lesson, and eat lunch later in the day. It ended up being like a party for all the parents who are not very highly valued. Everything was explained in poor English with some Thai names for food and traditional village toys. It was a really good way to get to know all the families.

For 'International Day' itself we are given a country to explore and celebrate for the day. One year my class had been given New Zealand

and there happened to be some rugby players from New Zealand in the area that I knew. I invited them in. One of the tasks for each class is to learn a dance from the country they are exploring. I knew the working-class Thai boys I teach would be reluctant to dance so I asked the rugby players to teach us all the Haka. I think outside the box, I know what my kids will like and I want them to feel happy in class. I know that the boys' parents used to be very poor. The fathers are mainly from the North East of England who came to Thailand for jobs in the oil industry and married women from Thai villages who might otherwise have ended up having very few choices of job. Now their children are being brought up in a good school, paid for with new-found wealth that is a new experience for them. School is a place many of these parents don't understand, so to include them like this is good for their children.

An unexpected outcome from the Thai parents' presentation morning was that when we were given Greece to study, they all came in to help. Being involved in their child's education is a new idea. 'International Day' has had the impact of building relationships with the parents and giving their kids a brilliant 'send-off'; it has brought the parents and the school community together.

Cassius Lubisi

My best experience of teaching was during the time of struggle when I worked in the underground of the ANC. My role was to be a teacher. I ran underground political classes to teach young people to analyse society at any time to support them in becoming leaders in the struggle. At any time the government could have come and arrested all of us so we had a strategy in the United Democratic Front (UDF) that at any given moment there should be three layers of leadership so that if the top layer was swept away layer two could take their place. So we had to constantly rebuild the layers of leadership. This meant that we had to constantly develop leaders. I am really proud that many of the people that went through my hands are now in serious positions of leadership. They all still say to me, 'Hey – you taught us politics and you taught us well'.

Another time I look back on with pride is when I taught at the University of Natal. My role was to undo all the previous education that the students had had which was designed to make them Black adminis-trators in the Bantu education system. They didn't like me as I was chal-lenging this. I used to be very strict with them and I took them through a very rigorous education. They didn't like the rigour at the time as they had never really been challenged but in the end they thanked me. When they left they said that I had encouraged them to be rigorous with their own students, to stretch them and to make them the best they could be. I still meet these students today and they continue to say thank you. I feel proud that I was able to take the bull by the horns and turn what had been a limitation into a strength.

Haana Sandy

There are two examples that I would like to tell you about. One involves teaching mathematics in the outdoors when I taught in Iran and the other describes the impact of me explaining my life history to students in England.

A newly qualified teacher in Iran has no say in where they are posted. I was sent to a girls' boarding school in a very small town which was quite a long way away from home. It was a disadvantaged and deprived town. I had been there for some time and in one of my classes there was a small group of Grade 11 girls who were ambitious and hard-working. They all dreamed of going to university and I was preparing them for all their mathematics examinations including algebra, geometry and trigonometry. In Iran there are three separate books to study, one on each of these areas. I usually used the big whiteboard to teach in the classroom but sometimes, when the weather was good enough and I didn't need a lot of whiteboard explanation, I took the group with a few mini-whiteboards outdoors.

On this particular day, I took them outdoors and we had a very productive group discussion exploring the mathematics which supported them in completing the exercises in the textbooks. I didn't have a detailed knowledge of the philosophy of learning outdoors, I was just developing my thinking about it but I thought it would be a good idea to discuss abstract topics in the outdoors and that it might help them to think and learn better.

The girls were eager to learn and curious to know about the world; they began to ask me questions about what the city I came from was like and what university was like. In breaks from their work they asked me questions about difficult issues in the world and I answered them with honesty. The setting made the girls more relaxed and we built up a bond. They opened up to me and trusted me. They made a promise to me that they would grow up like me and go to university. They said I really motivated and inspired them, therefore they wanted to be successful too.

I had a lovely head teacher at this school. We had a good relationship. She was supportive of my work and the relationship I had with the kids. She said I was humble, committed and hard-working and genuinely wanted to help disadvantaged students. This was one of the reasons she put me forward for a teaching award. Unfortunately, in most of the state's workplaces, especially in schools there are people watching and reporting people's words and actions to the regional Ministry of Education. I never received my teaching award. I was told that my hijab wasn't good enough for them and I was heavily criticised for my interactions with students. The fact that I was speaking my mind, openly and honestly, was difficult for them to digest. The state interpreted my open discussion with students about the world's and Iran's current affairs as poisoning and brainwashing students against the approved state view.

When I left the school, the girls promised me that they would work hard, and they gave me an ink-and-pen Farsi painting (Khataty). This form of art is important in Iran; originals by famous artists are expensive. They can take the form of a quote from a famous poet or a poem. An individual chooses the text and commissions an artist to create it. They chose a poem for me, framed in a wooden frame with all their names written on the back behind the frame. It was uplifting and emotional for me to receive this gift. The girls all promised me that they would never give up until they succeeded in going to university. I have never been able to find out if they did get to university or not but I think they will have done.

I have had several great experiences teaching at my current school. One of them is with a class who were very chatty and putting minimal effort into learning. One day, I told them very firmly that I was working hard for them. I told them, 'I'm fair, I listen to you and try to make the lessons interesting'. I told them that they were taking everything for granted and did not appreciate all of the facilities and my and other teachers' efforts.

I briefly talked about my background and my life story. They were really quiet and listened carefully. A few of them came to me individually afterwards to apologise. Two of them even wrote a letter saying sorry, signing off, 'from your newly transformed students'. Now they really appreciate my teaching style. A few girls have changed a lot and I tell them I'm proud of them when they ask if I am. So far, I am happy with the progress they are making.

Helen Toft

My best lesson has taken a lifetime to plan. It always takes me by surprise that I am at the end of my career but still get so sleepless, excited and full of ideas about how I might best go about leading a session, just like I did when I began teaching nearly 40 years ago. Shouldn't I be more confident, shouldn't it come more easily, shouldn't it all be at my fingertips? Maybe, but for me it's still a struggle, a struggle worth having, especially when I get feedback which helps me develop further.

In the spring of 2017 I was asked for the third year in a row to run a session at the Association for the Teaching of Mathematics conference entitled 'Journeys in Learning' with Tony and Dr Helen Williams, an early years mathematics specialist. I am not a natural early years teacher; any other age group I love, so to support my feelings of inexperience I asked the team if we could use a children's picture book about a construction site as the starting point. The book, *The Diggers are Coming* by Susan Stegal, is one that I know well from reading it to my grandson. I tend to try to plan significant starting points which will immediately engage but might also slightly unsettle learners. I often leave a space completely empty and build a drama from nothing as it were, or simply, but effectively transform a space. In this case, a circle of chairs in a conference workshop session in a hotel ballroom became a 'den' behind a huge roll of corrugated cardboard into which each colleague was welcomed. Everyone loves a den it seems, and they were willing to join the gang and have an adventure.

I took on what I call 'half role', which surprised even Helen Williams as in its truest form this sort of drama is normally framed very carefully in role. I introduced myself almost as myself, placing us all in role as part of an innovative social enterprise. My role was as the director of the social enterprise and I welcomed all members of the group as members of the board of trustees. This playful opening allowed me to 'gauge the social health of the group', something which Dorothy Heathcote, the inventor of such 'mantle of the expert' practice sees as vital. Tony and I have discovered that many teachers have a nervousness about mathematics, or drama, or both arising from their own school experiences. Our approach is that if we can share some fun together initially we might begin to chip away at our own and our students' blocks to learning, hence the playful 'seduction' to take part in the role at the beginning. I start gently gently. 'Who are you?' 'What do you do and why are you here today?' So far so ordinary but then I follow up with, 'What made you apply to be in our enterprise?' Those of the group who were experienced with drama were shocked at how quickly they could enter the role and they in turn enticed anyone not so experienced to enter the 'fiction'. I hope that this wasn't too difficult as my assumption was that the participants were already in it.

Helen Williams shared *The Diggers are Coming* and we virtually learned the book within the next few minutes. Next Tony focused on one page of the book, and on one image on the page, the caterpillar tracks of the diggers. The group had to design a giant caterpillar track out of the corrugated cardboard which would fit at least three of the group inside and would run along a grass track outdoors. The mathematics almost got lost in the fun the group had with this section of the session, but one of the main aims was 'team building' which was fulfilled with energy and laughter.

After a much-needed coffee break we came back into the hotel ballroom space to find a corner sectioned off with red tape. Inside that space I had laid out all sorts of buckets of pebbles, photos of children playing in refugee camps, coloured chalks and pens, dominoes and blindfolds – all stock-in-trade resources for a drama teacher. I shared the news that our enterprise had been asked to design an all-age playground for a new development of homes which would be totally inclusive, and support all those who visited in learning about the world with a focus on mathematics. The enthusiasm, imagination and creativity which the participants brought to this enterprise was fantastic; if only we had really been building a community playground.

At the end of this session Helen Williams reflected on the work we had engaged in during the session and reflected on how mathematics can be effectively taught through drama in an early years setting. All the group were asked what they would take away from the session.

After the session Tony received an email from one of the participants, Derek Ball, which has prompted a deeper dialogue about what was going on during the session. He wrote:

As I entered the cardboard space I was greeted in such a way that I was already in role: 'Welcome Derek, we are delighted to appoint you to our team, your application was very strong' and we introduced ourselves to each other with a mixture of personal sharing based on reality and the fantasy of the role. I wondered after why we were able to be so candid. We were invited to role play not someone else but ourselves. We were invited to wear a different pair of our own shoes. It occurred to me that every time I go into a classroom I choose, consciously or unconsciously, what role I am going to play. This session seduced us into a different pair of shoes from the ones we might have worn. This leads me back to thinking about phobias; perhaps we can overcome phobias by being seduced into a role in which the phobia does not seem so terrifying.

And I thought, thank you Derek, not only have you made me relieved that the session worked for all the hugely experienced experts in mathematics who were in the room, but you have given me a way to describe what I try to offer in sessions about what it is like to be a refugee. My best ever teaching session is about how to make a difference and how we can make the act of being forced to flee from your home seem not so terrifying. It allows me to hope that teachers can actually do something to support those who have survived such trauma.

J. Voytilla

It is supremely challenging to attempt to select what I think my best lesson might have been, more so because what exactly are the criteria for such an evaluation? Did the students score highly on a subsequent assessment? Did my planning of each lesson segment match the praxis of the lesson itself? Or did it simply just 'feel perfect' like the sublime satisfaction of when a football kick just 'flows' or when a bat hits a ball with that whack that seems to stem from your core? I am not really sure what the best criterion is, but I will share a story with you of one of my favourite lessons of all time.

This is from a time when my travelling school journeyed to the Galapagos Islands for three glorious weeks. I was able to teach 'lessons' completely free of classroom walls and I was unrestricted by any established curriculum – because I wrote the curriculum myself, based entirely on where we were, which was the ultimate goal of our school before committing to the International Baccalaureate Diploma Programme. This particular lesson was one of a series on evolution and species diversity – the most appropriate science curriculum I could fathom for such an amazing physical setting: where Darwin himself had once journeyed. The following was a blogpost that I wrote for parents afterwards:

> Today was an exciting ride into organised chaos ... not the whole day of course, just the crazy biological research at the end of it. But like the fractal patterns in the walls of an ammonite shell, it was a beautiful chaos – and one full of learning and utter amazement.

The day began as many others, breakfast, sea lion watching, and then classes from 9am to 12pm. Then in the afternoon, I took 26 students to the local dive shop to arm ourselves with what I called the *standard Galapagos science uniforms*, which consisted of a wetsuit, fins, snorkel and a mask, and then jumped on a bus with three national park guides and headed out of the city.

Destination: La Loberia ('where the wolves are')
Our Mission: to measure:

(i)   Terrestrial Species Abundance;
(ii) Sea Turtle Eating Habits;
(iii) The Relationship between Sea Urchin Abundance and Algae Abundance;
(iv) Aggressive Territorial Behaviour of Damselfish.

Crew: students, staff, Prof Luis Vinueza from USFQ (Universidad San Francisco de Quito), and three knowledgeable and friendly Galapagos National Park staff.

Organising a group this size for *real* research with only Luis (Prof Vinueza) and myself directing was *quite* a challenge. La Loberia is like a giant tide pool, or cove, which is like a socket along the island coast. Around 300 metres out the waves were pounding against the rocks that ringed us in and the surf was incredible. Prof Vinueza said that the best surfing in the Galapagos is on this island, and a couple of our guides admitted to surfing this shore. It was not massive like Hawaii but there *was* definite pipe going on out there [J. was suggesting that the sea was good for surfing!]. However, our research was based *in* the cove, not outside and so the incredible rolling waves soon became this surreal background for the science at hand.

To tackle so many research topics at once with so many people, we *had* to split the students into four research teams.

Group 1 was assigned to sea turtle feeding behaviours. Their research question was: *with what frequency do sea turtles feed, and what kind of algae are they feeding on?* This basically means that our student researchers stalked turtles in the cove and, armed with stopwatches, took notes underwater and recorded how often each turtle found would feed in one minute, and what kind of algae it was eating.

Group 2 was assigned to damselfish interspecies interactions. Apparently this fish is very territorial with its feeding area and has a feisty reputation for chasing off other grazers from its algal mats. This team's research question was: *what kind of behaviour do damselfish demonstrate to different kinds of competitive species?* This means that our student researchers hunted for damselfish and then, armed with underwater video cameras, captured interspecies interactions/fish fights for analysis.

Group 3 was assigned to sea urchin abundance monitoring. Sea urchins are voracious grazers and have been linked to areas of algal decimation. This team's research question was: *does sea urchin abundance/density have an inverse relationship with algal coverage?* This means that our researchers searched for sea urchin clusters and, by using an underwater quadrat that they brought from shore, measured the per cent cover of each cluster AND algal mat in order to calculate the ratio of urchins to algae.

Group 4 consisted of our non-swimmers for the day and since they had the longest trek ahead of them, we got them off first. Their mission was perhaps the most diverse of all. Their research question was broad in scope: *what is the feeding ecology and population density of iguanas and marine birds around La Loberia?* These researchers needed to explore along the coastline 1–4km ahead of our research base (La Loberia) and hunt for iguanas, mark their locations, measure feeding habits, population density and interspecies interactions. At the same time, they kept an eye out for marine bird species and performed the same analysis on them too!

So, where's the chaos? Deploying four research teams on diverse missions, clarifying objectives and variables, training student researchers on the use of materials and equipment, helping teams organise their research methodology, and all in record time to maximise our research window (low tide) and get our young researchers out in the water and on the trail! Then, trying to monitor each research team in the water and keep everyone out of the danger zone at the end of the cove. It was a beautiful kind of madness.

After about an hour and a half, our weary but glowing researchers returned to the research base from their particular endeavours, full of crazy stories of stingrays, turtles, humongous iguanas, strange and colour-ful fish and a few playful sea lions that decided to get up close and personal. Prof Vinueza walked up to me at the end, breathing hard but with a wild look in his eye and laughed:'I have never done anything this crazy before! I can't believe that it worked!' You see, scientists have a tendency towards slow methodical and meticulous preparation ... it's not often we get to run around being as science loco as our students!

Wait till he sees the mountain of crazy data we left him!

This particular lesson stands out to me because of the secret ingredient that I made sure we added to it: capital F-U-N. Normally, teaching young students about field-study techniques is challenging, and for many, not very engaging. Normally, it involves a bunch of string, a tape measure and a long and boring afternoon in some field somewhere, swatting bugs and counting an endless number of nameless weeds. This time, however, we had the chance to chase after animals, make some of our own tools, and spend the afternoon either snorkelling or clambering over rocky outcrops. Every single one of my kids wanted to keep going after the lesson had ended and the teachers too. Thus, that has become my criter-ion for a 'good lesson': learning works best when everyone is enjoying themselves and wants to keep on learning afterwards. 'What about the test results?' some may ask. Well, test results are arguably not the best evi-dence for authentic learning, but just to let you know, those scores were pretty darn high too.

Han Wei

I'd like to share two of my best lessons, one for adults and one for children.

The first one is for adults and the content is about teaching directions. This was a lesson I taught to tertiary level students in Nottingham. They were university students and we were doing some voluntary teaching as part of my MA studies in Teaching Chinese as a Second Language. We advertised the classes on Facebook and offered free Mandarin teaching once per week; this lesson was all about asking for directions.

My concept was to teach the pronunciation and characters first, and so I asked them to stand up and we practised together. The students fol-lowed my instructions, if I said 'go left' the students went left. I also asked them to repeat what I said. It was really fun. I had just recently taught the subject so some students couldn't remember the words or pronounce them properly, but doing the movement emphasised the memory and the body movements helped them to remember. It was about listening and speaking at the same time, and recognising the meaning and making the connections so they could repeat the movement. It was a lot of fun – especially when someone made a mistake! The next step was to use Google maps to ask directions. It was a Google map for the university so I used Google to show the university. I showed them the building we were in and asked them, for example, how to go to the swimming pool. With 'Street View' and the little person it meant that while they were telling me these directions, I was using the little figure to follow their instructions. It emulated real life and made them feel they could use the language. They were able to practise the language very effectively.

The best lesson for young students was last year when I taught my students at MCC (Manchester Chinese School). These students were 5–9 years old. We were learning basic pinyin (a phonetic representation of Mandarin using the alphabet combined with tone markers), pinyin is a tool to help people learn the correct pronunciation of Chinese. The first year of learning Chinese is pinyin year, then it's Year 1, Year 2, etc. The whole year is designed to teach students pinyin. I believed my students had the ability to learn more than pinyin. To spend the whole lesson on pinyin is a bit uninteresting. I designed each lesson. One of them included the basic pinyin and then they progressed to learn the combination of different vowels and consonants. Gradually they learned animal vocabulary relating to the combination and then gradually a small activity to practise what they had learned, using very short Chinese sentences. I believed it was more fun to do this, and they could manage this. I also believed they needed to learn pinyin, characters, vocabulary and sentences at the same time. First I introduce the vowels and consonants and they repeat; they also need to write the pinyin. Later, after learning the pronunciation and how to read and write it, I put the combination together. For example, consonant + vowel makes the word and I put them together to ask them to practise how to read it. Then I pick one word which is related to animals (most young students like animals and therefore it's easy to remember). This basic vocabulary helps them remember tones later on as they can refer back to these easy words. For each of the animal vocabulary I wanted them to learn I designed flash cards in black and white with pictures of the animals and they have pinyin and characters together with the pictures. Introducing the Chinese characters in this way enables them to learn them subconsciously. I expect they won't remember immediately, and they may not be interested, but one day when they see these characters it might ring a bell.

I select a picture at random and ask one student what it is. If they say it correctly, they get the picture. I make sure each student gets one or two pictures (and so far no one has not got a picture!). The picture is in black and white and in the break they can colour it in. I believe that as they colour it in they are subconsciously practising the pinyin and characters and learning that way. Some of them did some amazing things when they coloured them in, such as colouring a rabbit with the blue sky, birds, flowers and grass. Some of them have rainbows and more rabbits. They are very creative.

After this, I collect all the pictures back and show them to everyone so they can see each other's creations. In this way we are reviewing the vocabulary. I then give each of them one or two pictures back randomly, so they may or may not get the same ones they coloured in. Then they have to present the animals. I ask, 'Who is rabbit?' or 'Who is frog?' and they stand up, show the picture to everyone, and say 'I am the rabbit' in Chinese. This helps them say the sentences and practise pronunciation and grammar. By listening to each other they are also learning the meanings and the vocabulary.

All these things help them to remember the basic pinyin vowels and consonants, but makes it more interesting, and makes it more than just a pinyin class. I'm very proud of my students and they have a really strong foundation in pronunciation due to these classes.

Reflections

As we looked back over these narratives we were struck by the humanity which came through in all the memories. There was a sense of teachers putting their beliefs into practice and of being able to remain true to themselves, as human beings, even when they took on the role of teacher. We see this particularly strongly in Haana's story; and the importance of teaching in and shaping a new and more just society is evident in Cass's narrative. In contrast to Chapter 8 these narratives illustrate the importance of teachers treating learners as human beings, as equals. These are examples of person-centred education at its best. Emotions are allowed to take centre stage, are expected to be and are seen as central to the learning process. Han illustrates how important it is that teachers believe that all learners can succeed. For Cass, this is vital as his students will be taking leadership roles in a future national administration; for Tony he wants to get past walls which may have been built because of previous bad experiences in learning mathematics.

All these lessons have been planned very carefully, not necessarily through filling in a long and detailed proforma, but from drawing on previous experience to make sure that we use our practice to plan the very best new experience for a particular group of learners we are working with. Helen describes this as 'taking a lifetime to plan'. In a sense, every new lesson that we teach draws on all of our prior experience and so takes a lifetime to plan.

Many of the lessons draw on authentic contexts for learning. We hear of soap operas taking centre stage; of great political ideas being brought to life in a current context; of the finest children's books, both fiction and non-fiction being used and of Google maps providing an instant resource. The ivory tower does not appear in these lessons. The narratives all bring the outside into the classroom. Ed's narrative describes the excitement and motivation of the parents in involving themselves in their children's education when he literally brought the outside in.

There is a sense of fun, a sense of playfulness and of variety and creativity across these narratives. There is also a serious side to the playfulness. Serious play if you like. These narratives show how teaching and learning can transform the world of the teacher and of the learner by building a community of learning beyond the walls of the classroom. Our best lessons are aspirational for our learners and for ourselves. They suggest a lifetime dedicated to learning as well as an understanding of lifelong learning.

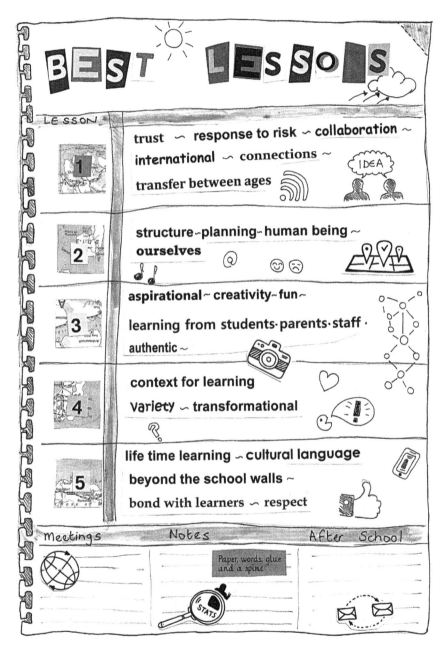

Figure 9.1 Graphical summary: Our best lessons.

Commonplace book: Entry 9

What is your biggest success in terms of teaching someone else?

Why do you think you remember this over other things? What made it so successful from your point of view?

How do your know you were successful?

Part 4

Visions for education

My aim is to produce students who will leave school with the ability to look the world in the eye and say, 'I am here; this is what I can do: If you accept me then the world and myself will be enriched; if you reject me it is your loss as well as mine'.

(R. Ridley, Head teacher of Halifax High School
writing in Scottish Drama 5. 1996)

This final section revisits the narratives that have made up the bulk of the book to offer the co-authors' vision for a global education system. As a way of bringing the book to a close we analysed all the narratives for common themes and drew these together to first imagine what an ideal global education system might look like and second explore and share the skills and competencies teachers in this global system would need.

Chapter 10

Our vision

The book was written in the order in which it appears. First, we wrote the introductory chapters to research and share the context of international education around the world. Then we shared our autobiographies and our working days. We moved on to share our stories of experiencing education as learners and as teachers. At each point, we read each other's stories and shared these stories with our co-authors. So, the book has been constructed by reading, redrafting and rereading the narratives that we have shared with you. This meant that we had to write collaboratively – we would spend writing days together as a core team reading to each other and finding a quiet space to write, or in Ed's case to draw.

And so to this final section. We now had all the narratives in the book and wanted to draw on them to put together our vision for education at a global level. We reread all the reflections that close each chapter and looked at the graphics which offer an alternative summary. As always, we took turns to read the reflections, pausing between each reading to jot down notes on the issues that were resonating for us. Then we talked and talked. The results of these conversations follow.

Our vision for an ideal global education system is an education system which adheres to the following principles:

- It is collaborative: within educational settings collaboration will be seen as central. Teachers will collaborate with teachers, jointly planning and teaching groups, sharing their expertise and learning from each other. Learners will also collaborate. While students work in mixed-attainment groups diversity will be seen as a strength as learners share skills and experiences to learn and develop together. Diversity will be evident within the teachers. The norm will be for teachers to have experience across a range of cultures and understandings from a range of backgrounds. Learners will collaborate across age groups and technology will be used to facilitate collaboration across national boundaries. Schools will be sites of collaboration with the wider school community. Parents and other members of the community will collaborate with teachers to support the education of all learners in the school.

- It is authentic: teaching and learning will be authentic. Authentic materials are used to support the learners and teaching is authentic in that relationships both with learners and between learners and the teacher are based on mutual respect and trust. Learners take responsibility for their own learning and enjoy the freedom they are given to engage in learning. Assessment is authentic. That is, that assessment measures intellectual accomplishments that are worthwhile, significant and meaningful. Assessment tasks either relate to the way that skills are utilised in the real world or focus on asking students to show their understanding through the performance of key skills.

- It builds communities: students will, within this system and through education, build new communities in which they feel at home. All learners have a sense of belonging within the school and are supported in building a central core of values and beliefs. Education acknowledges both family history and a shared national history within a global context. Conditions for learning are carefully constructed within the school and learners feel secure and able to take risks within this supportive environment. Learners welcome challenge and have the confidence and self-belief to challenge themselves.

- It expects movement: there will be movement on a local scale and on a global scale. Learners will move around the learning space finding appropriate areas for learning and sharing their learning with all that they share educational space with. Learning spaces and learning plans will be flexible – change will be expected. There will also be movement out of school both to learn in the local environment, in the wider national context and across countries, either virtually or literally. Learners will understand that learning can come from being exposed to new cultures and learn to embrace and celebrate difference as offering alternative viewpoints.

- It uses a range of spaces and places: learning will take place in a wide range of spaces and places and will not be confined to the single classroom in which we learn for most of the year. There will also be a range of technological spaces used to enhance and facilitate learning. Any space or place that is accessible to learners will be a place for learning. This means that all those with whom students engage across this range of spaces will be seen as teachers, allowing learners to learn with teachers from cultures from all around the world in order to discover new worlds for themselves.

- It is supported by expertise: teaching is seen by teachers and learners as a craft and teachers and learners revel in subject-specific expertise and creative expertise. Teachers have expertise both in subject disciplines and in pedagogy. Theory is understood as central to understanding learning and theory is evident in practice. Key theories that form the spines of subject disciplines are explored and understood by learners.

And finally: our vision is of an education system which is inclusive and underpinned by love.

Commonplace book: Entry 10

Reread the reflections on each chapter for yourself.

Look again at the graphics which conclude each chapter.

Use this rereading to support you in developing your vision of My Ideal Education System

Chapter 11

What makes a global educator?

To complete the book, five of the authors met around Helen and Tony's kitchen table in Yorkshire, UK, with Ed Emmett joining virtually from Bangkok. We met to think through the set of skills and competencies that a 'global educator' who was working in a school which adhered to the vision for education we described in Chapter 10 would require. Ed Walton joined us to complete the final graphic.

As with previous chapters our starting point was to read the vision from Chapter 10. Having revisited this vision our discussion focused on the questions:

- What defines an educated person?
- What skills, knowledge and understandings would this educated person have?
- What experiences may such a person have had at school?

We offer the results of our discussion as a series of bullet points.

To open the discussion, we described to each other what we understood by education in its broadest sense. We explored the attributes we would use to describe an educated person. We shared what we saw as the most important outcomes of education.

What defines an educated person?

- They have something to say and can communicate their ideas.
- They take responsibility for their own learning.
- They can think critically and independently.
- They are excited about learning. They revel in their ignorance.
- They are responsible citizens.

- They are open-minded and open to new experiences.
- They are accepting of difference in a positive way. They understand there can be different points of view and that these diverging views are starting points for discussion.
- They are open to taking risks and can adapt to new situations.
- They work to develop their local communities and the wider society of which they are a part.
- They continue to learn from life experience.
- They can apply their knowledge in their everyday life.
- They enjoy thinking about and focusing on new experiences such as eating an exquisite meal, climbing a new route, participating in theatre, or art, or designing landscapes.
- They are inquisitive. They never stop questioning and are always asking, 'what's next?' They are always moving forward.
- They are excited about the possibilities tomorrow brings.
- They don't make snap judgements. They see beyond stereotypes.

To help us to reflect on how teachers could support individuals in becoming 'educated', we moved on to discuss the sorts of skills and understandings that such an educated person would have.

What skills, knowledge and understandings would such an educated person have?

- They can ask pertinent questions. They are able to dig deep to find the information that they need to answer questions that they have.
- They are 'awake', aware of the world around them and the ways in which it is changing. They look and see with open eyes.
- They listen carefully, read thoroughly and research skilfully to answer questions that are important to them.
- They are flexible.
- They can think for themselves. They have the tools they need to think through problems they encounter and to resolve issues.
- They have good research skills.
- They are good listeners.
- They have good communication skills and can communicate well whether this is through writing, talking or presenting.
- They can understand and critique data whatever form it takes. They question and critique views of the world given in mainstream media.

- They understand their bodies and understand themselves.
- They can come to an understanding of the world around them through accessing core knowledge about the world.

Finally, we analysed these discussions to explore the sorts of educational experiences that would be needed in order to educate such an individual.

What experiences might such an educated person have had at school?

- As a precursor to this list we acknowledged that an educated person may not have had all these experiences at school. Indeed many of us had our most formative educational experiences outside classrooms.
- They will have taken part in community experience or volunteering in the community.
- They will have taken responsibility for caring for the school environment or for the local environment.
- They will have taken part in an active school council or been part of a community organisation.
- They will have learned in non-hierarchical settings.
- They will have taken pride in the settings in which they have learned.
- They will have learned in global settings and from global educators.
- They will have been taught by parents and other members of their community.
- They will have travelled, either literally or virtually, to experience how they adapt and respond to different situations across a range of cultures.
- They will have made presentations in order to communicate their ideas to their peers and to adults.
- They will have researched questions which are important to them.
- They will have made mistakes and adapted the way that they work or their awareness as a result of these mistakes.
- They will have taken risks and been supported in order to take these risks.
- They will have learned across a range of disciplines in order to make connections between curriculum areas.
- They will have used a wide range of resources including new technologies.

- They will have experienced being cared for and will have cared for others.
- They will have had the opportunity, and been expected, to think in different ways.
- They will have had the opportunity, and been expected, to communicate in different ways.
- They will have had the opportunity to encounter and learn with/ from a variety of people. They will have encountered difference and learned from this experience.

This leads us to ask what sorts of teachers these educated people have had. Asking this question allowed us to think about our own teaching practices and explore ways in which we would want to develop ourselves to become the best global educators we could be.

What skills and competencies would their teachers require?

1   They will have a deep understanding of the subjects(s) that they teach both in terms of knowledge of the content and the strategies that can be used to support learners in developing understanding(s) of that content.

- They find common themes to make connections within the subject and across subject boundaries.
- They draw on a range of techniques from a variety of subject disciplines and apply these appropriately in a range of curriculum areas.
- They accommodate, and expect to develop, a range of learning styles within their classrooms.
- They are up to date in terms of recent research and developments in the subjects in which they teach.

2   They will have well-developed interpersonal skills enabling them to work collaboratively with learners, other teachers and members of the wider school community. They show unconditional positive regard for all those they teach and their carers.

- They give active support to learners and colleagues.
- They empower learners to take control over their learning.

- They challenge inappropriate behaviours. They are not afraid to say 'no' to learners and colleagues when necessary.
- They see all learners as individuals and see it as important to respond to individual needs.
- They are respectful and respected.

3 They take responsibility for their own professional development and for the development of those they work with.

- They take risks in their own practice to develop as a teacher.
- They set themselves professional development goals seeing themselves as lifelong learners.
- They see feedback from learners, colleagues and other members of the school community as positive and use it to reflect on their practice.
- They value knowledge in others and draw on this to support their own development.

4 They make a difference both to the lives of the learners in their care and to colleagues they work alongside.

- They develop and maintain networks which can be used for support and development.
- They create shared goals for the future with learners and colleagues.
- They see themselves as agents of change and work collaboratively to make change happen.
- They understand how power operates within the education system and work to develop non-hierarchical approaches to education.

This brings us to our final image – our shared image (see Figure 11.1) of what makes our ideal global education system.

Figure 11.1 Our vision of a global education system.

Commonplace book: Entry 11

It is appropriate that the final words in this book should be your own.

Examine the list of educational experiences we believe could contribute to an 'educated' person. Which of these opportunities does your current institution provide? Are there any you don't currently provide which you could offer in the future?

Examine the list of teacher competencies. Divide this list into three under the following headings.

Competencies I already have

Competencies I could develop quickly

Competencies I need to develop over a more extended period of time.

And finally draw or find an image which for you encapsulates 'global education'. Add it below.

References

Cotton, T. (1998) *Thinking about Teaching*. Oxford: Hodder and Stoughton.

Dearden, J. (2015) *English as a Medium of Instruction—A growing global phenomenon: Phase 1 interim report*. London: British Council.

Forster, E. M. (2005 [1927]) *Aspects of the Novel*. London: Penguin Classics.

hooks, b. (1999) *Talking Back: Thinking feminist, thinking black*. New York: South End Press.

Mason, J. (1987) 'Only Awareness is Educable', *Mathematics Teaching* 120: 30–31.

Woolf, V. (1958) 'Hours in a library', in *Granite and Rainbow: Essays by Virginia Woolf*, pp. 24–32. New York: Harcourt, Brace.

Index